CW00685715

IN A LAND OF FOREST AND DARKNESS

THE HOLOCAUST STORY OF TWO JEWISH PARTISANS

SARA LUSTIGMAN OMELINSKI

ap

ISBN 9789493231344 (ebook)
ISBN 9789493231337 (paperback)

Copyright © 2021 Yossi Millo and Batya Omelinski

Translated from Hebrew by Karen Dinur

Publisher: Amsterdam Publishers

info@amsterdampublishers.com

In a Land of Forest and Darkness is **Book 11 of the series Holocaust Survivor Memoirs World War II**

All Rights Reserved. No part of this publication may be reproduced or transmitted in any form or by any means, electronic or mechanical, including photocopy, recording or any other information storage and retrieval system, without prior permission in writing from the publisher.

CONTENTS

Prologue   1

1. Wedding and War   5
2. Roots   12
3. The Courtyard   23
4. From Calamity to Holocaust   33
5. The Heart of Darkness   56
6. Hunted   92
7. Polesia Woods   128
8. Homeward   152

Epilogue   186

Testimony of Misha Omelinski   189
The Silent Bug   247
Kind Request   253
Holocaust Survivor Memoirs   254
Holocaust Survivor True Stories   257

Dedicated in loving memory to my parents, David and Batya Lustigman, and to my sisters Yehudit and Nekhama, who perished in the Holocaust

PROLOGUE

My sister and I grew up in Israel in the 1950s, children of Holocaust survivors. We were a family of four—no grandparents, aunts, uncles, cousins, nieces, nephews, or in-laws. It was just my mother, father, sister, and myself. At the time there were many families just like ours, so it didn't seem out of the ordinary. Now that I am a grandfather myself I know how great our loss.

Our parents, unlike many other survivors, told us much of what they had gone through. In fact, we were their captive audience: in the young Zionist state of the 1950s, people didn't want to hear about victimized Jews. I believe our parents' fighting with the partisans may have made it somewhat easier for them to share their experiences because they were not sullied by the ugly stain so prevalent in public discourse back then: they did not go like "lambs to the slaughter."

And so we heard about the Holocaust more than most kids our age. My father mostly recounted heroic deeds, battles against Nazis, ambushes, sabotage operations, and a life of freedom in the forests. My mother tended to tell us bits from here and there, stories about life at home, in the town, and later in the forests. Her stories were vivid and not too terrifying, but we sensed from a young age, and certainly as we grew older, that something dark and terrible—even monstrous—lurked beneath the surface. We didn't ask too much. We didn't probe.

Years later, in the 1980s, I started to work as a translator and editor in addition to my regular job in computers. One of my first assignments was to edit annual research volumes published by Yad Vashem, the World Holocaust Remembrance Center in Jerusalem. For three years I edited dozens of articles and studies on the Holocaust and was exposed to the most shocking and horrifying accounts. I became immersed in the subject, almost against my will. Even so, I evaded my mother's repeated requests to help her write down her story. I was simply afraid. Only in 2010, when my mother was living in a home for the aged and my father had been dead for ten years, did I agree to do so with a heavy heart.

I had originally intended for her memoir to be an internal document for our family, something we could pass on to our children and grandchildren and that future generations might read some day, hopefully gaining some understanding of what their ancestors had gone through and what their lives were like. But then I realized that if I wanted my parents' story to be read, it would need to be organized, accessible, and written in the style of a memoir. Fortunately my mother's stories needed only very minor editing. She had a wonderful memory and a flair for making her story come alive, and she spoke with such confidence, fluency, and attention to detail that all I needed to do was to sift, order, and arrange. And of course, I changed nothing of the stories themselves.

This is a family project. My sister Batya initiated the whole thing, as she too felt that our parents' story needs to be preserved. She helped tremendously with all her heart and resources, suggested useful ideas, read early drafts, helped in editing and proofreading, and was heavily involved in the design.

We can only hope that this book will be read for many years to come, not only within the family, but by a wider audience. I know this is what my mother wants.

In May 2011 I happened to hear a lecture titled "The Holocaust and Cinema" by a historian from Yad Vashem. One of the examples she presented was the opening scene of Claude Lanzmann's 1995 documentary *Shoah*. It turned out the scene had been filmed in Włodawa—the Polish town where my mother had grown up—and in it the director interviewed a Polish resident about the fate of the town's Jews. Suddenly I saw the streets of Włodawa, even more rundown than I remembered from my 2003 visit. The Pole pointed to the houses that had belonged to Jews and recounted their names. Afterward, at the town square, a number of local residents surrounded Lanzmann and, feigning innocence, he asked them, "So what happened to the Jews?" One woman looked straight into the camera and said with a steady and determined voice, "They were resettled."

It was at that moment that I realized the only way to understand the Holocaust is through the testimonies of the survivors themselves. Each and every Holocaust survivor has a story, and it is a story worth telling. Each is the story of an ordinary person, like you or me, who became entangled in one of the most terrifying and stormy events in history. This is the story of two such families, of two such towns, and of a world that no longer exists. It must not be forgotten.

- Yossi Millo, Israel

1

WEDDING AND WAR

September 1, 1939 was a beautiful day in Włodawa. Although it is true that war broke out that day far to the west, we were having a wedding and were joyful. My aunt, Eva Chervonogura, my mother's sister, was marrying Meir Zilberschatz of Lublin. Even though war was imminent, I don't remember being overly worried. On the contrary, having just turned fifteen, my adolescent mind figured it might just be interesting. I imagine the adults must have been quite worried, however. Grandpa Shaya even made a few shady business deals just in case. And at school we were instructed what to do in the event of a gas attack. Of course, no one could have predicted what would actually happen.

Memory is an elusive thing. After more than seventy years, some of my recollections are clouded. Some images remain with extraordinary clarity, while others have all but disappeared. For the memories I have lost, there is no one left to ask.

I had graduated elementary school that year and was studying for entrance exams for the local high school, the

Gymnasium. However, chances were slim that my parents would have allowed me to attend even if I had been accepted. The school no longer allowed Jewish students to miss days for the Sabbath and holy days, and since my parents were religious, failure to observe those days was out of the question. In fact, my older sister, Yidiska (Yehudit), attended the local high school for two years and then was sent to a private commercial school in Warsaw after the local school canceled its special dispensations for Jewish students.

That same year, I was seriously ill until shortly before the wedding. I was bedridden for close to two months due to a tooth infection that caused my left cheek to swell enormously. At a certain point, I could barely breathe. We all waited for the pus to drain and the swelling to subside. Meanwhile, I was fed liquid food through a straw, stayed home from school in bed, and spent hours twirling my hair, which had grown very long. The swelling finally disappeared, and one day I went with my mother to Brest-Litovsk,[1] some fifty kilometers north of Włodawa and the closest city to our town. It was the second time I had ever left Włodawa since I was born. The first time, three years earlier, was to visit my father's family in Sokołów Podlaski.

In the city, after visiting the dentist and having my tooth extracted (using ice for anesthesia), we went shopping for fabric for the wedding. This was especially exciting for me as I have always loved clothes and fashion. The shops did not carry readymade clothes in those days. People would buy fabric and have a dressmaker sew the garment according to the client's measurements and the latest fashion. I clearly remember the fabric Mama and I chose for my dress: a dark blue chiffon with white polka dots. It was airy and wispy. Yidiska thought it brought out the blue in my eyes.

My mother, Basha (Batya-Khinka), was an impressive woman. She stood straight and tall and was always well dressed. No wonder I was always proud to be seen with her when we went out. She had a clear complexion and long brown hair that she wore in a bun. Although she was sickly and suffered from various maladies, she was an excellent housekeeper and ran the house meticulously and tastefully.

Needless to say, the dresses were ready in time for the wedding. Guests for the wedding had arrived from Warsaw, Sokolow, Lublin, and the surrounding area. Some stayed with relatives in Włodawa, while others stayed with us. Our house was bustling. The bride, Mama's younger sister, Eva, was in her thirties, which was not considered young in those days. She was shapely, tall, and always elegantly dressed. Eva met her husband-to-be, Meir Zilberschatz, through a matchmaker, as was the custom. He was a decent, upright fellow from a fairly wealthy Lublin family that made its living in the grain trade. Until then we hadn't really gotten to know him well, but I do recall that he would go swimming in the river every morning.

I don't remember too many details of the wedding itself. I do recall that the veil was white, but the bride's dress was not! Instead it was a lovely pale blue. There was a *klezmer* musical group and lots of dancing. Men and women danced separately, as was the custom of the Gerre (Gur) Hasidic community to which Grandpa Shaya belonged. It was a joyous occasion. The music, the setting, and the gathering of family and friends all added to the festive atmosphere. The ceremony was held at Grandpa Shaya's house, under the *chuppah* (the traditional wedding canopy) erected on the spacious second-floor porch, which was also where we built our *sukkah* (a temporary booth) every year for the holiday of Sukkot (the Feast of Booths). The porch had a glass wall running the length of the house. Below, one could see the garden where large tables had been set with white tablecloths and the most delicious wedding feast would be served. After the wedding, two tables were set every day for seven days and the town's poor were welcome to partake at any time of day.

The next day, life was back to normal for the most part. However, because of the war, many of the guests had a hard time getting home as train service throughout Poland was disrupted. Some guests were stuck at our house, while others found themselves stranded en route. The war was foremost in everyone's mind.

Our house was part of a compound that also included a flour mill and a power station that supplied electricity to the whole town. Because of those facilities, it was commonly believed that our area would be targeted for bombing and we had best get prepared. Since our yard was paved, we dug zigzagged trenches in Aunt Tova's garden, which was outside of our compound, beyond Zabagonie Street. In case of an air raid, we were supposed to run there. In the end, the Germans didn't bomb the whole town, only the areas on the other side of the Bug River, targeting the train station and a bridge over the river. There were a couple of air raids that were close enough to send us running to the trenches in Aunt Tova's garden. Each time it happened, I was so frightened that I had the worst stomach pains imaginable.

It wasn't long after that we learned that, despite initial optimistic predictions of the Polish propaganda and newspapers before the war, things were going badly at the front. The town became inundated with soldiers, vehicles, and horses. Each day more and more soldiers could be seen moving east, retreating from the advancing German army. There were waves of refugees pouring into town as well. Many came to our house, were offered food and drink, and told us their stories. The weather was still fine that month, almost as if to mock us, although we prayed for rain to stop the bombing.

Not long after, we started to hear the thunder of cannons. The front was getting closer. Soon, a large battle was being waged near Włodawa.[2] We no longer sought shelter in our trenches but rather in the cellar beneath the power station, which seemed safer. When the siren sounded, all of us—including the workers—ran to the cellar.

One day at noon, the cannons stopped firing. All was quiet. We sat and waited, but nothing seemed to be happening. Finally my sisters and I suggested that we take a look outside. Mama would not hear of it. There was no way that young girls should wander about outside where the place might be swarming with enemy soldiers. She wrapped her large kerchief around her head and went out herself.

She went into the house and couldn't believe her eyes. The Torah scroll had been taken out of the holy ark that our father had built in the office, been unrolled, and was strewn on the floor of the long hallway connecting the three wings of the house. Even though German soldiers were present, Mama didn't hesitate for a moment to start rolling up the scroll. The soldiers looked on—some sneering and mocking, others simply staring out of curiosity. None harmed her. When she was finished, she wrapped the Torah in her kerchief and hurried back down to the basement.

Apparently it was deemed safe enough to go upstairs. I remember that after I left the basement, I saw a crowd of German soldiers, half naked, washing themselves using bowls they had taken from our house.

Our compound was the only place in the town with running water. That was the first time I had ever seen German soldiers. These were the Wehrmacht forces that had occupied the town. I thought they were all very handsome. They were tall and blond with blue eyes, and were clean, disciplined, and well outfitted. What an impression they made!

Eastern Poland 1939

1. The Jews referred to Brest-Litovsk as Brisk Delita, or in short, Brisk. It gained renown as the site of the signing of the peace treaty between Russia and Germany on March 3, 1918 toward the end of World War I.
2. One of the last battles the German army waged against the Polish army took place near Włodawa. The Polish soldiers of the Polessia Division fought bravely and surrendered only at the end of September 1939. Many weapons were abandoned in the area and peasants gathered them up and hid them. Most of the stash was later handed over to the partisans.

2

ROOTS

Today Włodawa is a small town on the western bank of the Bug River in Eastern Poland. However, in the 1930s, Włodawa was a typical Jewish shtetl. The Bug now marks the border between Poland, the Ukraine, and Belorussia, [1] but until September 1939, the area to the east of the Bug was also part of Poland. The town has been in existence since the twelfth century, but otherwise has no outstanding features except the elegant synagogue, one of the most beautiful in all of Poland, which was built in the eighteenth century.[2] Until the Holocaust it had a large Jewish population. In fact, on the eve of the war, there were 5,650 Jews, about two-thirds of the total population. And just like similar towns at the time, it boasted a vibrant and rich Jewish culture. There were synagogues and religious seminaries, theaters, cinemas, community services, sports clubs, newspapers, political parties, shops, and other businesses.

Our whole extended family lived together in one large compound and in two additional houses nearby. The compound included residential areas, a power station, a flour mill, workshops, cowsheds, gardens, and a large yard. It extended for eighty meters between two parallel streets: Zabagonie and Folwarczna.[3] The property was jointly owned by three partners—my maternal grandfather, Shaya (Isaiah) Chervonogura, who owned 20 percent; Moshe Spokoyne, who owned 25 percent; and Mordechai Gurfinkel, who owned 55 percent. All three partners lived in the compound with their families.

Włodawa Synagogue, July 2003

Grandpa Shaya was born around 1870 in the town of Zambrów. He made his fortune during the First World War by trading with the Germans, which is also how he learned their language. After the war, in the 1920s, Grandpa relocated to Włodawa, and with the other two partners bought the large compound from a Jew who was planning to emigrate to Palestine. The power plant had already been built in 1908, and by 1913 it was supplying electricity to the whole town. Supposedly, the first electric light bulb in all of Włodawa was installed in the synagogue. The flour mill was built soon after and was run by electricity supplied by the power plant.

Apparently business was good. Grandpa was a shrewd businessman and ran the business (and his family) with an iron fist. He was forceful, opinionated, excellent at trade, and a well-known figure in the area. Involved in local affairs, he donated to charity and once even held the position of head of the town council and council member. He sported a short reddish beard and was a heavy smoker. People said he was difficult, but he also had a reputation of being honest and fair. Even his employees liked him. When it came to his granddaughters, there were no girls more loved and spoiled—especially me.

Since Grandpa Shaya was a follower of the Gerre Hasidic sect, our family was pious—you could say ultra-Orthodox —but not the most extreme. On weekdays, the men wore ordinary clothes and round hats with visors. Only on the Sabbath did they don a *Capota*, the traditional long black silk coat of the Hasidim. The women dressed modestly, but stylishly and elegantly, and didn't shave their heads and wear wigs. They were very observant when it came to religious law, Sabbath regulations, and kosher food laws —no compromises were tolerated. And, of course, the girls were closely monitored and kept far away from "bad or unsavory influences."

Our paternal grandmother, Khaya-Itta Lustigman, was even more extreme than her son and daughter-in-law. She would check what books I brought home from the library ("What? Dostoevsky?"). It got to the point I would lock my books in a cabinet, away from her prying eyes. Nor were we permitted to go swimming (possibly they feared we might drown). Not to mention that someone would tell on us if we were seen talking to a goy. Heaven forbid!

Grandma Rivka, Grandpa Shaya's wife, was efficient and very active, unlike Mama, who was slower and more thorough. Grandma was very observant and wore a wig. Every morning before school we would have breakfast at Grandma's—sweet rolls with butter, jam, *halvah* (a dense, sweet sesame confection), and milk—all freshly delivered and delicious.

* * *

Grandma Rivka and Grandpa Shaya had five children: Batya-Khinka (Basha)—my mother, born 1896—was the oldest, followed by Yitzhak-Meir (Itche), Tova, Hava (Eva), and Avraham (Avremele). When the girls—Basha, Tova, and Eva—were of marriageable age, a suitable match was found, and the young couple would then receive a house in the compound or nearby. The same was true for the boys, except that each son and son-in-law also received a job or business opportunity either within the compound or nearby. Thus, the whole family remained together.

Of the five siblings, four were married: Tova married Berl Alberstadt and had one daughter, Bella. Itche married Khaya-Sara from Maków-Mazowiecki; they had no children. As discussed earlier, Eva married Meir Zilberschatz the day war broke out. Avremele was the youngest and hadn't yet married. Upon Avremele's finishing military service, Grandpa Shaya set him up in a glass-cutting business where he sold window panes and mirrors.

My mother, the oldest, was married to David Lustigman from the town of Sokołów Podlaski. My father, or *Tata,* didn't come from a wealthy family, but he was considered a good match as he had been a brilliant student and was an ordained rabbi.

He belonged to a Hasidic group originating in Kotzk.[4] He was born in 1893 and had a delicatessen in Warsaw before their marriage. After the wedding, he continued to run his deli and came to Włodawa only on weekends until he finally received a house in the compound and went into business with Uncle Itche. They ran a plant, which was also in the compound, where they produced fine flax oil as well as a cheaper oil. I remember Tata previously tried his luck at a different endeavor—leasing fishing rights at a lake and selling the fish. However, that business failed, and he lost quite a bit of money.

David Lustigman, Sokolow 1915

Tata was smart, well mannered, good hearted, and generally well liked. He was also known for his keen sense of humor. One time a tax inspector came to check Tata's accounts. I was sitting there at the desk, working on my stamp collection or some other hobby, when the inspector asked Tata whether he had any assets that were not listed in the books. "Yes, I do," he replied. "I have three daughters. They are my treasure."

Nor do I recall him ever getting mad at us—well, except for one time, after which I ran off to Grandma Rivka's.

He had two older brothers and many relatives. My sister, who was going to school in Warsaw, met quite a few of them and used to tell me about them. [5]One of the brothers had emigrated to Palestine in 1935, which is how we came to have family in Israel. We would occasionally get letters and photos from them. Tata's parents, Grandpa Moshe and Grandma Khaya-Itta Lustigman, lived in Sokolów and made their living from a small restaurant on the ground floor of their house. I never met Grandpa Moshe, but once I did meet his elderly mother, Great-Grandma Mina, in 1936, when I was twelve and we traveled to Sokolów to meet Papa's family.

Grandma Mina had reached the age of ninety-four by then. She was tall and stood straight, dressed all in black with a black lace headscarf. When she heard the commotion we were making she was alarmed and asked, "Who died? Who died?" She calmed down when someone told her it was David's children who had come to visit. Her eyes lit up, she smiled, and gave each of us girls her blessing. To this day I remember a distinct old-lady smell that emanated from her.

* * *

Later that year, my paternal grandmother, Khaya-Itta, came to stay with us from Sokolów. Both her husband Moshe and his mother, Mina, had died by then. Khaya-Itta had no one left in Sokolów. Of her three sons, the eldest, Boaz, had died. The second, Yaakov, had emigrated to Palestine and also had died. Her third son, David—my father—had moved away to Włodawa. So she came to live near him. She was in her seventies, short, always elegantly dressed, educated, and energetic. She brought with her an antique black wooden chest with metal ornamentation. The trunk contained silver dinnerware and valuable religious and ceremonial articles that had been passed down from generation to generation —Hanukkah menorahs, special boxes for *etrogs* (a fruit used in rituals during Sukkot), candlesticks, and more. This chest of valuables would have particular significance later on.

The Lustigman daughters, May 1928: Yidiska (back), Nekhama (right), and me

Today I have children, grandchildren, and great-grandchildren of my own. But at that time my sisters and I were the youngest members of our family, the last in the family line. The three of us were born in Włodawa, at home, where a midwife was called in to help with the deliveries. I was born Sara (Surele) Lustigman in 1924, the second of three daughters. Yidiska (Yehudit) was born two years earlier and Khumka (Nekhama) two years after me.

When I was twelve, I discovered that I had a brother who died in infancy. His name was Yehuda, and Yehudit was named after him. Nobody had ever mentioned him before; I found out about him when, while I was sick, I came across a photo of a baby I didn't recognize in one of the family photo albums.

My sister Yidiska was a real soulmate and the one with whom I had a special relationship. She was so kindhearted, patient and devoted, a wonderful human being. We both looked like our father physically (whereas Khumka looked more like our mother) and at one glance you could tell we were sisters. Yidiska was outgoing and sociable. She had a lot of friends, both boys and girls. Although an average or above average student in most subjects, she displayed quite a talent for math. When the dispensations for Jewish students were canceled in the Gymnasium at Włodawa, our parents sent her to study in Warsaw at a Jewish college specializing in commerce. In addition to Hebrew, English, and Latin, the curriculum included practical subjects, which pleased Grandpa Shaya, as he apparently intended for her to take part in running the business.

My relationship with Khumka was not as close, mostly because she was younger and I had such a close relationship with my older sister and her peers. When war broke out, Khumka was about thirteen years old, good-looking, friendly, sociable, and cheerful. She perhaps was spoiled as the baby of the family. Khumka was enrolled at the Beit Yaakov school for girls,[6] but she rebelled against what she considered their over pious ways and so she was sent back to the regular school.

My family was politically affiliated with the Mizrahi Zionist movement. Aside from uncle Itche, who was more Orthodox and opposed to Zionism, my father, mother and all their siblings were Zionists. In 1932, about two years after I had started learning at the regular Polish school, a branch of the "Tharbuth" school[7] was opened in Włodawa. After it received official government recognition, many of the Jewish children went there full time.

I didn't transfer to the Tharbuth school in order not to disrupt the school year, but I did go twice a week in the evenings. The school was located on Sokolów Street, in the center of town, and there I learned Hebrew, Bible, and Hebrew literature and poetry. On the Jewish holidays they held ceremonies, parties, and festivities. Class photos from that time are now on display at the Jewish Museum of Włodawa, which is in the old synagogue.

I remember receiving a letter from my cousin, also named Sara Lustigman, from Palestine. In the letter, she included the words to a popular local song, "We Are Building a Port." I brought it to Hebrew class and we learned to sing it together. The regular Polish school was also a place where I enjoyed learning: I was a good pupil and particularly liked my teacher, Jerzy Filip.[8]

Looking back at this photo of the three of us, taken in 1936, I see three sisters from a good family, two years apart, standing next to each other as in formation, looking straight into the future; Three girls with everything to look forward to, surrounded by a loving and supportive family, with no reason on earth to suspect they were facing catastrophe.

The Lustigman sisters, 1936. From left: Khumka, me, and Yidiska

1. I have referred to places as they were called at the time. Thus, Belorussia and not Belarus.
2. The synagogue was built in 1764 in Baroque style. Fire destroyed its interior in World War I and again in 1936. Both times it was restored. During the Nazi occupation it was used for storage, and under Communist rule as a fishing club. Today it serves as a Jewish museum and is a popular tourist site.
3. The street names Zabagonie and Folwarczna were changed to Kraszewskiego and Jasna, respectively.
4. This Hasidic movement was founded in the eighteenth century by Menachem Mendel Morgensztern of Kotzk, better known as the Kotzker Rebbe (1787–1859).
5. The two brothers were Boaz and Yaakov Lustigman. Boaz died sometime after he married; his son and wife perished in the Holocaust. Yaakov was a Zionist, and in 1935 he emigrated to Palestine with his wife and their two daughters, Rivka and Sara. Yaakov died of cardiac arrest before the war in Tel Aviv. Rivka

married Yehuda Rabin and they had two children. Yaakov's second daughter, Sara, settled in Kibbutz Sarid and had three children.

6. A chain of Orthodox schools for girls, founded in Poland in the early twentieth century.

7. A chain of Zionist Hebrew schools which operated mainly in Poland.

8. Shortly after the war broke out, as part of a policy to eliminate Polish intellectuals, he was deported to Auschwitz and perished there.

3

THE COURTYARD

A very spacious courtyard lay at the center of our compound, which was home to three extended families—and the center of my life growing up. Our lives were richly entwined because of this living arrangement.

My immediate family, the Lustigmans, lived in the home that stood to the left of the gate. It was a one-story brick house with three wings (the kitchen, living area, and office; the office was used by Grandpa, although he lived in another house), a basement, and an attic. The basement included a storage area, a pantry, and space for cold storage. A long hallway connected the three wings, with each having a separate entrance preceded by a small fenced-in area. There was a chicken coop outside the kitchen, a flower and vegetable garden outside the living area, and wild chestnut trees outside the office wing.

The spacious kitchen had a wood-burning stove, shelves crammed with dishes and jars, and a large dining table with a wide bench. At night the bench was turned into a bed for our maid, Helenka. She was a pretty Ukrainian girl from one of the neighboring villages who helped with all the household work, cooking, cleaning, and childcare. When my sisters and I were little, Helenka would take us to pick flowers in the fields. When we got older, she taught us all sorts of things about which we couldn't tell our parents.

The living area had a substantial dining room/living room with a large table, a cabinet where the fancy dishes were displayed, a sofa, a bookcase for prayerbooks and other holy books, and an imposing desk with many drawers. A porcelain heater ran the length of one of the walls. My sisters and I all shared one large bedroom.

Grandpa's office also served as a synagogue. Tata had built an ark for the Torah, and on Sabbath, the Hasidic community members of Sokołów and others would pray there. A large wooden counter divided the office in two. Grandpa was on one side and four employees were on the other—a cashier, two accountants, and a clerk. Grandpa would work during the morning, and at noon he would rest on the bench in the kitchen.

Our house was considered modern by Włodawa standards in the 1930s. We had running water in the kitchen, landscape paintings and tapestries on the walls, ceiling lamps with electric light bulbs, and curtains and wooden shutters covering the windows. The floors were of polished wood and painted red. We had no indoor toilet (although there was one in Grandpa's house, which even had the extra luxury of a toilet seat), and there was running water in the large bathroom. The office had one of the few telephones in town and, besides its obvious use for the business, was an invaluable means for customers to report an electrical power failure. I enjoyed it too. Some evenings I would phone my friend, Rachel Holtzman. Her father was a wealthy lumber dealer, and they, too, had a phone.

Grandpa Shaya Chervonogura and his business partner, Mordechai Gurfinkel, shared the second house: a two-story building behind ours. A non-Jewish caretaker named Zaremba lived in the basement with his wife and daughter, Jadwiga. Jadwiga was a bright and talented girl. During the war she was sent to the women's concentration camp, Rawensbrück, and survived. Zaremba was our "Sabbath goy"—doing things on the Sabbath that Jews were not permitted such as turning lights on—and our guard. His duties included closing the gates, locking the wooden shutters, and sweeping the yard. His wife milked the cows and did housework in the compound. A total of eight people lived on the first floor: Grandpa Shaya and Grandma Rivka, and Mordechai and Gittl Gurfinkel and their four children.

The upper floor was occupied by three of Gurfinkel's unmarried siblings: Irena, Marissa, and Shimon (Shimek). Another of his brothers, Yaakov, was already living in Tel Aviv at the time. This was the building having the wide porch, with glass enclosing the walls and ceiling, where the marriage canopy was erected for Aunt Eva's wedding.

A large fruit orchard stood between the back of the house and the wall. I especially remember the fragrance of the jasmine and lilac bushes and the large round flowerbed where reddish-purple peonies grew. All of us children in the compound would play in the garden or just get together there. On hot days, Gurfinkel's unmarried sisters and brother would put on bathing suits and spray water on each other with the garden hose. That was certainly an unusual sight in those days: workers and people passing by would just stand outside the fence and stare in amazement.

There is much more to tell about the large Gurfinkel family and their friends. Doing so will help paint a clearer (though not complete) picture of the men, women, and children who populated the landscape of my childhood.

One such person was Irena, Mordechai's sister. She was a unique young woman with her stylish, short haircut in the latest European fashion. And she wore pants, which was a novelty at the time. She also had pajamas and all sorts of modern garments, and she smoked incessantly. An opinionated and liberated woman, she had many lovers and a large dog named Prince, who wreaked havoc on the garden. Her sister, Marissa, was plump and generally well liked. She was engaged to a non-Jewish pilot, but he was killed when his plane crashed. As a symbol of mourning, she wore a black armband as was customary among Christians. In fact, the Gurfinkels were meticulously secular. They didn't even speak a word of Yiddish.

Gurfinkel's youngest brother, Shimek, was about twenty at the time. He was a really nice fellow, witty and friendly. I thought he looked like the actor Danny Kaye. He had a gorgeous girlfriend named Nekhama, who had worked as a model in Tel Aviv while Shimek was serving in the army. She returned to Poland when her father was dying. During one of the air raids in September 1939, I didn't manage to get to the trenches at Aunt Tova's in time and remained outside in the courtyard. There I ran into Nekhama. I was petrified and suffering from severe stomach cramps, but she seemed totally relaxed. She said she believed in fate, so she wasn't running to the shelter.

While the bombs were falling that day, Nekhama told me her whole life story.[1]

With profits from their shares in the family business, the three siblings didn't have to work to support themselves. They lived a free and easy life, with ski vacations and trips abroad, and money to spend on clothes and other extravagances. Shimek even bought himself a car—in those days you could count the number of private cars in Włodawa on one hand. Shimek didn't have much use for the car in town as the roads were mostly unpaved, but he took us kids on road trips in the area.

Mordechai Gurfinkel had four children: Mania (the oldest) was the same age as my sister, Yidiska—pretty, though not particularly bright. In 1939 she married Moshe Lichtenberg, who later became a commander of a group of partisans. Fella was one year my senior and a dear friend, and Avraham and Lola were both younger than me.

Yidiska (left) and me

The Spokoynes lived in the third house, a wooden structure with a slanted roof to the right of the entrance from Zabagonie Street. It looked modest from the outside but had five rooms, a kitchen, and small bedroom for the maid. Moshe Spokoyne and his wife had three children: from oldest to youngest, they were Shlomo (Solomon), Mendel (Moniek), and Binka. My sister Khumka was older than Binka. Moniek was close to me in age, a handsome, blond-haired fellow and a good friend. Solomon, who was Yidiska's age, was blind. When it became apparent that he was very musical, it was arranged for him to study the violin with the klezmer musician Spielman, and he later was accepted to the Warsaw Conservatory and the Institute for the Blind in Vienna. After the Anschluss (when Germany annexed Austria), Solomon returned to Włodawa. All the neighbors would gather to hear him play during vacation. He had several blind friends and a girlfriend, a chemistry student, who was also blind, having lost her eyesight due to an explosion in the chemistry lab.[2]

Imagine my surprise when we visited Włodawa in 2003 to find the Spokoynes' wooden house still there. It was abandoned, but solid.

The houses and the families were the heart of the compound, but the businesses there were the heart of Włodawa. The compound was situated at the edge of town, not far from the fields, and was completely fenced in, with gates for pedestrians and carts situated on the two parallel streets Zabagonie and Folwarczna, which at that time were unpaved.

The flour mill, July 2003

The Lustigman Family compound, July 2003

Amid the dwellings, shops, and other businesses stood the most impressive structure of all: the flour mill. It was a three-storied red brick building and boasted the first and only elevator in Włodawa. The mill operated on electricity generated by our power station, which was also built of red brick and stood behind the mill.

I later learned that the authorities had tried to expropriate it many times. Their attempts were thwarted only thanks to untiring efforts and determination and with the influence of powerful connections. The power plant was steam operated: wood was transported to the station by wagons and burned in order to heat water in boilers. The resulting steam propelled a turbine, which in turn produced electricity. Each wood-laden wagon came in through the courtyard, where it was weighed on a scale in the ground—first upon entering and again upon exiting—thereby determining the weight of the delivery and the amount to be paid. In charge of the weighing was one of the partners, Moshe Spokoyne. The plant's chief technician was a Polish man, Kaminski. The plant engine ran nonstop and its hissing noise could be heard day and night. At times, if the engine broke down at night, we would be woken by the sudden silence, which was both strange and wonderful. The silence didn't last long, however—it was broken by the sounds of urgent voices, telephones ringing, and technicians being called in to repair the engine.

Tata and Itche's plant for oil production stood behind the power station, but it was later relocated and replaced by a glass workshop and warehouse belonging to Uncle Avremele, who had been released from the army.

* * *

The last summer before the war was a very happy one. I was growing up and felt mature for my age. Yidiska let me join her in all sorts of outings with her friends. We hiked and took bicycle trips until one time I fell and was injured. From that time on, I stopped riding. There were other activities, though. One time, Khaya-Sara, who was married to Uncle Itche, told us that Itche was going away on business and that she too would be away, and we could make use of their house for a few days. As soon as our uncle left for the train station, two of Yidiska's friends came over and the four of us settled in on the porch. The boys played the guitar and the mandolin and we sang. We felt so grown up and reckless. Suddenly the gate flew open: Itche was back—he had missed the train. The two boys panicked and ran off, and Uncle Itche, who was extremely devout, made a scandal. But Tata wasn't ruffled. "Leave my daughters to me," he said.

The courtyard was truly the center of my world at a time when I was no longer a child, but not yet an adult. The place was always bustling with the comings and goings of clients, farmers, tradesmen, workers, and, of course, friends. Needless to say, I don't remember them all. Many years after the war, in the summer of 1991, my late husband, Misha, and I visited Włodawa. We entered the courtyard at Folwarczna Street. At the gate sat a guard who looked to be about fifty years old, and we asked if we could go in.

"Who are you?"

"I am Chervonogura's granddaughter," I answered. "We lived here before the war."

He was dumbstruck. "Which one? Yidiska? Surele? Khumka?"

That came as a surprise.

"Surele," I said.

We could see that he was touched. "I am your neighbors' son, the Mitch family. I remember all of you. You were big girls; I was just a little squirt."

31

Of all the Jews who lived in the compound, hardly any survived the Holocaust. The survivors were gone too, dispersed throughout the world. Three extended families were destroyed within the space of a few years—and with them a whole world, the world of my childhood—simply vanished.

---

1. Nekhama had two brothers and a sister in Palestine. Both brothers were murdered in the 1929 massacres in Jerusalem. Her sister had a mental breakdown and remained hospitalized until her death in 1934. The sole surviving family member was another younger brother, who emigrated to Palestine in 1940. Nekhama and Shimek married shortly before the war, also before the death of her father. A year later Nekhama and Shimek had a son, and the three perished in Sobibor.
2. Even the Germans recognized the talent of this virtuoso violinist and left him alive for some time, having him perform at various events. He was killed in the final roundup. His father and Moniek were hidden by Poles in the village of Wyryki and survived.

4

FROM CALAMITY TO HOLOCAUST

September 1939–June 1941

On September 1, 1939, the day of Aunt Eva's wedding to Uncle Meir, Germany launched an invasion of Poland from the west, the north, and the south.

On the 17th, the Soviets invaded from the east in accordance with the notorious Molotov-Ribbentrop Pact to partition Poland between them and the Germans. The last battle ended with the remaining Polish forces being totally encircled southwest of Brest-Litovsk, not far from Włodawa. On Sunday, September 18, the Germans occupied our town. Although the German army remained in Włodawa only for a short time, they would end up leaving their mark of terror.

Life went on in early September after the Germans took over Włodawa for the first time, with shops open, and to all appearances, business proceeding as usual. Uncle Avremele returned from the war—he had been serving in the Polish army but deserted the first chance he got and came home. In the early days of the occupation, a number of Jews were killed by German soldiers, but the murders appeared sporadic and random.

Then, one day, German soldiers entered the compound, with the S.S. paramilitary organization, the S.D. security force of the Nazi Party, and the Gestapo secret police not having reached the area yet. They started shouting "*Männer Juden raus* [Jewish men out]!" I was standing there in the courtyard and saw soldiers herding together all the men from the compound. Tata ran downstairs and a soldier ran behind him, shouting "*Schnell! Schnell!* [Hurry! Hurry!]" They took all the men, among them Grandpa, his partners, Tata, and Uncle Avraham, and locked them inside the synagogue along with many other Jewish men from the town. The Germans threatened to set fire to the synagogue with the men inside unless they were paid a large sum (*kontrivucja* in Polish, or ransom). They had no food, water, or decent ventilation. No one was allowed near, although some food and water were smuggled in at night through the rear windows. After three horrifying nights and days, the community managed to raise the ransom money and the men were released.

But the terror didn't end there. Fifty of the most distinguished townsmen—those who were wealthy, renowned, or in leadership positions (according to a list provided by the Polish police)—were taken out of the synagogue. They underwent a cruel, brutal ordeal. Grandpa Shaya was one of them. When he returned home, he told only a little of the abuse to which he had been subjected. I learned what happened only later, from another victim who had also been taken, Yekhiel Greenhouse.[1]

First the soldiers took almost all their money and belongings, leaving each man with only twenty zlotys. The prisoners were forced to do exhausting physical exercises and work, and then they were loaded onto a closed truck and taken to the prison in Chelm. All the while they were beaten viciously and subjected to humiliating and demeaning shouts and insults. Each prisoner was locked inside a cell, and one at a time they were brought into a large and dimly lit interrogation room in which there were a few S.S. men and a large table. They were ordered to get undressed and were whipped mercilessly. Many lost consciousness. The whippings lasted the whole night. After suffering the most horrendous beatings, they were returned to their cells, bruised and half conscious. In the morning, they were led to the train station and ordered to go home, using their remaining twenty zlotys.

It suddenly became clear that this was a totally new and different situation. A heavy and oppressive atmosphere enveloped the whole town.

And then, suddenly, on Yom Kippur Eve, all was quiet. The Germans disappeared, and for a few days there was no ruling power. The Polish government had collapsed, the Germans had gone, and the Soviets had not yet arrived. The Poles dubbed that period "interregnum."

All the Communists emerged from hiding, donned red arm bands, and started to run the town as if the Messiah had arrived. Here and there they took revenge on suspected enemies. A few days later, the Soviet army entered Włodawa.

Compared to the clean and disciplined German soldiers, the Soviets seemed like a wild bunch. Their uniforms were tattered, dirty, and old. Their vehicles seemed like dilapidated and outdated rattraps, and they certainly didn't behave like military men. They descended upon the streets like locusts, looking for merchandise and hungry for Western goods, the likes of which they had probably not seen in the Soviet Union for quite some time. They had a particular appetite for clocks and watches and were willing to buy any timepiece offered to them, even if old or out of order.

But it was soon clear that the situation would change again and the town would return to the Germans. During the Sukkot holiday, we were all gathered in the sukkah on Grandpa Shaya's porch eating our meager meal of canned food. Suddenly, there was a knock on the door and three young fellows came in. Grandpa invited them to join us, and one, the son of Kletzki, a photographer, started a long speech. He praised Mother Russia, Papa Stalin, and Communism. He then tried to persuade Grandpa to take the whole family to the Russian-controlled area east of the Bug. The Soviet army even promised to provide trucks and transport our belongings. Throughout his speech the family listened in total silence. No one interrupted; no one argued. After all, who knew who would rule here tomorrow? But no one expressed support, either. The adults knew what likely would happen if we stayed under Soviet rule—they could deport us all to Siberia as enemies of the party and the workers' class. And besides, how could we leave our homes and property and venture into the unknown? "We will not be refugees," Grandpa declared. His word was final.

Many Jews, however, were convinced that the Germans were worse than the Soviets—especially after the synagogue incident—and that they would be better off moving east. Most who left were Communists; Young and adventurous people with no particular roots in the town; those who were poor and convinced the Communists would not harm them; or Jews who believed what happened at the synagogue was a sign of things to come.

In retrospect, it is impossible to know whether Grandpa made the right decision or an enormous mistake. Many of the Polish Jews who escaped to Soviet-occupied territory were, in fact, deported to Siberia, where they remained for the duration of the war. They suffered terribly and many died of hunger, disease, or hard work. Most, however, survived. Those who were not deported to Siberia, including most who enlisted in the Soviet army as it retreated, found themselves under German rule two years later or prisoners of war and were subsequently killed in Russia, Ukraine, and Belorussia.

On September 18, the agreement regarding the border between Russia and Germany went into effect. The town of Włodawa west of the Bug would revert to Germany, and the smaller town of Tomaszowka and the train station east of the river would be under Soviet control. I happened to be at the market square on that day and witnessed the official ceremony marking the transfer of power. Soldiers from both armies stood at attention, and then the red Soviet flag was lowered and the Nazi swastika raised in its stead. Two officers saluted each other and shook hands, and the Soviet troops left in a long column eastward. It would take two years for Stalin to pay for his treachery; the price would be unbearably heavy when the Germans invaded. As for us, we were under the control of the Germans, and nothing would ever be the same.

In mid-November, the military government was replaced by a civil one and Włodawa was incorporated into the province of Lublin, in the *Generalgouvernement*, the part of occupied Poland that was not annexed directly to the Reich. The Wehrmacht troops were replaced by S.D. forces commanded by a man named Richard Nitschke.[2] They set up headquarters in the most beautiful house in town, situated on the main street, Pilsudski Boulevard,[3] right opposite the school and municipal sports field. In addition there were all sorts of policemen, including Polish and Ukrainian regulars.

My memories of the German occupation include all sorts of people who came and went, drastic changes in our lives as a result of the occupation, and certain specific events that I can never forget. Many of my memories are chronological, but some are not, like snapshots scattered in an album.

A short time after the onset of the occupation, Yossl Weller, a relative on Tata's side, arrived in Włodawa from Warsaw. His father, Shmuel, had gone to America before the war and had managed to settle there and arrange for his family to join him. He had even procured the necessary immigration documents and tickets for the journey. The trip had been booked for September 1, the same day it turned out that the war broke out, however. That meant that the Wellers were stuck in Warsaw. Not only were they stuck there, but they lost everything in the heavy bombing of Warsaw. And so it was that he came to stay with us. Yossl had been a pious yeshiva student, but meanwhile had become less religious.[4]

He was a pleasant fellow, always ready to help out and grateful for whatever anyone did for him. We all liked him a lot. Especially Yidiska. In fact, the two of them fell in love. Tata lost no time in writing to Yossl's father in America, saying he approved of the match between the two and asking his opinion. Previously, with the outbreak of war, the elder Weller had periodically sent us packages from America with all sorts of dry goods—sugar, coffee, cocoa, and so on—and we would sell everything to the *Judenrat* (Jewish council set up by the Nazis) so they had foodstuffs to give the Germans. The money we received was used to buy basic provisions like flour or sugar, which we sent to the Wellers in the Warsaw Ghetto.[5]

At about the same time, a *Volksdeutscher* (an ethnic German) from western Poland arrived in Włodawa and announced that all the businesses and residences in the compound belonged to him. It appeared that shortly before the war Grandpa Shaya had made a fictitious deal with the man, with the two other partners' consent. Grandpa had experience with the Germans during the previous war and felt certain they would expropriate property belonging to Jews. Therefore he made a deal with this German whereby ownership of the whole compound, with its businesses and dwellings, was transferred to him, with the understanding that after the war the property would be returned to the partners. The German also guaranteed that while the agreement remained in effect, all the residents would be allowed to remain, and that all the partners would receive a certain sum of money, which would be enough to live on.

It was not to be. The Volksdeutscher broke the agreement almost immediately. One by one we were forced to leave our homes. First, he took over all three wings of our house —the office, the kitchen, and the residential wing—and we moved in with Uncle Itche. Soon, he demanded that all the other residents leave. Grandma Rivka and Grandpa Shaya and all the other partners and their families were forced to find other places to live. Needless to say, the Volksdeutscher did not provide an income as stipulated in the agreement. Thus, we found ourselves with no means of support or income. The whole Jewish population of Włodawa lost their businesses due to regulations enacted by the new government.

A number of other anti-Jewish regulations went into effect almost immediately. Jewish businesses were expropriated, with most transferred to Ukrainians. Jews also were no longer permitted to hold any public job with the city or government. The Polish mayor, Alexander Behr, was replaced by a Ukrainian. The Judenrat was established in late April 1940 (Grandpa Shaya was asked to join but refused).

One of their first tasks was to supply the Germans with living quarters and anything else deemed necessary. Next, the Germans demanded forced laborers for various jobs. A Judenrat representative went to the S.D. headquarters and managed all Jewish affairs according to the instructions he was given by the Germans. As a matter of course the Judenrat arranged easier jobs for relatives and close acquaintances.

For example, twelve of the town's best young men were assigned to the sanitation department, but one day, the commander, Nitschke, summoned them to his office, stood them in a line, and informed them that from then on, they would serve as the "Jewish Police." Those twelve young men had no choice but to serve as policemen for the Germans, against their will. They were outfitted with truncheons, armbands, and caps.

Within a few short weeks, the whole Jewish population was almost totally destitute. Nevertheless the Germans continued to demand more money.[6] All business connections and most personal relationships with Gentiles had become illegal and were ended at once. So to provide some sustenance for the Jewish population, the Judenrat was permitted to open what was called a "Cooperative Store" where Jews could trade in coupons for provisions. The shop didn't carry much—some bread, potatoes, salt, and yeast, which was all distributed in small portions. Up until 1941, some supplies reached Włodawa from the "Joint" organization in Warsaw and were distributed at the Cooperative.

More and more decrees were publicized on large placards in a number of locations in town. It was prohibited to have a radio, bake bread, or buy or sell or conduct business of any kind with a Gentile. All Jews had to wear a white armband with a yellow Jewish star on their sleeve upon leaving their houses; all had to take off their hat to any passing German soldier or police; all were prohibited to walk on the sidewalk. Any infraction was punishable by death.

It was the same throughout Eastern Europe. Religious Jews were subjected to especially humiliating treatment. They were forced to dance and sing, and were filmed doing so. Their beards and sidelocks were cut off in public to the sounds of laughter of German soldiers and police. One day, Tata came home from town and half his beard had been cut off.

The Lustigmans, 1941. From left: Yidiska, mama,
Khumka, Tata, and me

In the few photos remaining from that time, I see the armbands turned downward at the elbows so at least they would be hidden from those walking behind. I also remember Tata remarking wryly that the visor of his cap was broken because he had had to remove it so many times. In this photo which was taken in front of Uncle Itche's house, probably at the beginning of 1941, Mama and Tata are looking dismal and solemn while we girls are still smiling.

I remember another alarming and dreadful event from that terrible winter. Around December 1939, two Ukrainian peasants showed up in town and reported what they had seen in the forest near the train station adjacent to the village of Sobibor, a few kilometers south of Włodawa: many wounded or dead soldiers, who appeared to be Polish by their uniforms, were sprawled on the ground.

Immediately a delegation was formed. When they arrived at the site, they saw that the victims were Jewish soldiers who had been taken prisoner. The group of over a thousand men had been transported by train to the Sobibor Station, ordered off the train, and then machine gunned. About half were killed. The survivors escaped into the forests, but by the time help arrived, they either froze to death or lost fingers or limbs to frostbite.

The Jewish community of Włodawa immediately organized. Sheets were collected from all the houses to use as burial shrouds. Makeshift hospitals were set up in public buildings, seminaries, and houses of worship, and the town's Jewish physician, Dr. Adam Shpringer, tended to the wounded as well as he could. Many women, including Yidiska, volunteered to nurse the patients. Some soldiers who eventually recovered remained in the town and were adopted by Jewish families. Our family hosted two of these men every day for dinner: the Sternberg brothers, aged 27 or 28, from Szczuczyn in the vicinity of Bialystok. When Tata learned that the two were Hebrew teachers, he was extremely pleased as that meant they could teach us Hebrew so as not to forget what we had learned at Tharbuth. However, our Hebrew lessons stopped when the system of forced labor began.

Meanwhile there was no school, and we looked for some way to pass the time. Mama suggested that I learn a trade and Tata offered to teach me bookkeeping, but I wasn't interested. In the end, they sent me to be an apprentice with an accomplished seamstress from Warsaw, Sara Schneiderman. Rather than teaching me the trade, however, the dressmaker had me do household chores as if I were a maid. I rebelled and returned home.

One day, I happened to be walking down the street when I recognized my best friend from school, Danusha. She was a Polish girl of my age and lived on Folwarczna Street, not far from me. We used to wait for each other every morning before school and went many places together. We always did our homework together, and I helped her a lot, so I was a welcome visitor at her house. "Danusha," I cried with my arms open wide in anticipation. "Danusha!" But she ignored me completely and walked past, her eyes blank as if I did not exist.

Sometime afterward, the decree regarding forced labor was announced. Each Jewish man and woman between the ages of fourteen and sixty was required to work. The new officer in charge of the labor force was a tall, thin German named Bernhard Falkenberg, who had moved to Włodawa with his wife and son. He wore leather breeches and boots and always carried a whip. He moved into Aunt Tova's house, which was outside the compound, and set up a mechanism to make the most of the Jewish workforce.

Since there was not any real work in the area of Włodawa, Falkenberg decided to drain swamps. He soon had a force of two thousand men and women from the town working in teams, with a boss in charge of each team. It was well organized. The laborers worked hard and received bonus food coupons. Falkenberg was a strict manager but also quite fair, and they said he knew all the workers by name. Grandpa worked in his yard, where he tended a greenhouse for vegetables. Tata and Khumka found work at the cooperative store: Tata handled merchandise and Khumka was a salesgirl.

Khumka, 1942

Thanks to connections, Yidiska and I were lucky to get work with a Volksdeutscher from Western Poland by the name of Antoniewicz, who had also arrived at Włodawa around that time. He oversaw the forests in the vicinity of Włodawa and had received permission to employ Jewish laborers. About forty women and girls worked for him in the plant nurseries, where he grew saplings. Occasionally Yidiska and I worked in Antoniewicz's private garden. We worked every day except Sunday, from 7 a.m. to 7 p.m. Antoniewicz was also fair to his workers. Mama would come at noon with lunch for us. While we worked, we sang popular songs, and I learned quite a few in Yiddish. The work itself was not difficult, but it could be humiliating, especially for a girl like me from a privileged family. I remember once when I was sent to bring seedlings from the shed in Antoniewicz's yard. Since we didn't have a horse, I pulled the cart myself through the town, embarrassed to be seen pulling a cart full of plants in full view of everyone.

A few of the girls I worked with became lifelong friends. The three I remember best were Sheindele Lederman, Andje (Channa) Edelsberg (one year younger than me and a pupil at the Tharbuth school), and the beautiful Peska Bornstein.[7] I recall how, early in the war and before the edict requiring armbands, Peska and I would take a walk on Pilsudski Boulevard on Sundays and sometimes the street would be full of German soldiers ogling us. We couldn't stop laughing; those dumb Germans had no idea we were Jewish.

Antoniewicz's plant nursery, where we worked, was near a former Polish army camp, now being used by the German army. From the nursery we could see the camp in the distance. We observed what looked like army training activity, but when we got closer we could see that the soldiers, though wearing German army uniforms, did not look German. There was something Asiatic about them.

One day, probably during the latter half of 1941, one of the soldiers threw a stone our way. I picked it up and saw a note wrapped around the stone, but in a language I didn't recognize. We were all baffled. Then somebody glanced at it and realized it was in Russian. "My mother knows Russian," I said. "She studied Russian in high school." Later at home I showed the note to my mother and she translated it: "Hello girls. What's the name of your town? What country is it in? What precinct?" and other questions like those. Mama wrote a note in Russian answering their questions, and the following day we tossed the note back to them, wrapped around the stone. That incident puzzled me for a long time, and only after the war did I learn that the soldiers had in fact been Soviet POWs who had agreed to serve in the German army rather than starve to death in a German POW camp. The training we had seen in 1941 was army training.[8]

Such events, which were entertaining or at least interesting, were rare. We mostly occupied our minds with basic survival, including that our diet had deteriorated. In exchange for our work, we received coupons that could be redeemed for a specific amount of bread per day, available at bakeries in the town. To supplement our diet, I planted a small vegetable garden at our uncle's house. We even kept a goat that provided us with milk—sour and not tasty, but milk just the same. Fortunately, Grandpa Shaya had connections with some Poles he would encounter in Falkenberg's yard, where he did maintenance jobs. Grandpa would trade all sorts of items that we had at home—for example, items from Eva's dowry—for foodstuff. And Mama would bake bread at home, despite the Germans having outlawed it. There was a German named Luther who would patrol around town with a gigantic German shepherd on a leash, trained to find Jews baking bread. Whenever he and the dog appeared on the street, in an instant the street would empty out, all the Jews panicking and fleeing in all directions, as it would attack a Jew the moment its owner shouted *Jude* over bread and other offenses. Heaven help those who were caught. Mama's bread remains in my memory as the most wonderful delicacy, as was her homemade jam.

That winter, Yidiska's health began to decline and she had difficulty working. Mama also developed health problems, and at one point she had a skin fungus on her hands and could not bake. That was why I learned to bake bread, a skill that would prove useful later when I joined the partisans. It was amazing: the weaker my sisters and

47

mothers became, the stronger, more mature, and more effective I became. And I had not even turned sixteen.

Admittedly I didn't feel quite so brave when I encountered Luther on the street one time with his German Shepherd. I had just come out of a house, and there they were in front of me. I froze, scared out of my wits. Luther scrutinized me. The dog sat and waited. Time stood still. Finally, Luther said in German, "Where is your *Judenschandebande*?", meaning literally "shaming band," which was what the Germans called the armband that Jews were required to wear. It was folded around my wrist, and with trembling fingers I undid it and wrapped it around my arm in its proper place. Luther looked at me for a moment and then turned and walked away.

Hunger was gradually becoming more severe. Our family was managing relatively well, although our meals were becoming less and less sufficient. Once, as I lay in bed in my room, I saw a shoebox on top of the wardrobe closet. My curiosity got the better of me, and I climbed on a chair and took the box down. When I opened it, I saw that it was full of raisins that Tata was saving to make wine for Pesach. Tata always made excellent homemade wines from various fruits, and normally we would have a few bottles of his wine in the pantry. I took a handful of raisins and ate them with greedy pleasure. I never told anyone, but every few days I would help myself to another handful of raisins until one day, I opened the box and it was nearly empty. A few days before Pesach, Tata discovered that the wine raisins for the holiday were gone and naturally asked each of us who had eaten them. Yidiska and Khumka denied everything, and so did I. To this day I feel guilty about what I did, but my hunger was so great and the temptation so strong, and I was, after all, a child.

Sometime later, the agreement that Grandpa and his partners had made with our Volksdeutscher, the one who took over our compound, entered a new phase and Grandpa Shaya ended up in prison. It turned out that not only had the scoundrel broken the agreement and taken possession of the partners' property, but he had also cheated the authorities. He had established a factory for producing soap and candles but had neglected to get a license and not paid the authorities. The fact it came to light meant someone probably had snitched. During the ensuing investigation, information regarding the illicit fictitious agreement was revealed and the Volksdeutscher was thrown into prison along with two of the partners. Grandpa had gone into hiding at a neighbors' house, the Mitch family, who lived on Folwarczna Street. The investigation continued, and one day, two German S.D. officials, Hammer and Genze,[9] showed up at the courtyard to search the compound. As they hadn't found evidence elsewhere, they entered our house, overturned the desk, and emptied it. They examined each document, and if it wasn't to their liking, they became enraged, threw it down, or tore it up. Suddenly they came upon a drawer that was locked. "Whose drawer is this?"

"It's mine," I answered, my voice trembling.

They ordered everyone except me to leave.

"Open it!"

I brought the key and opened my secret drawer, the one in which I always hid my personal things from Grandma's prying eyes. They glanced at the photo album, discarded the diary I had just started writing, and from the bottom of the drawer took out a suspicious looking document. It was illustrated and the writing was strange. "What's this?"

I didn't know so I went out of the room and asked Mama what it was. I went back in and told the soldiers it was a *ketubah* (Jewish marriage certificate), but I didn't know how to explain what it was, especially in my halting German. They tore it up, threw it on the floor, and angrily left.

While Grandpa was in hiding with the Mitch family, someone would always bring him kosher food from home. But after a while, Grandpa suddenly showed up at home, late at night, and said he just couldn't hide any more. He had decided to turn himself in. Despite efforts to dissuade him, the following morning at dawn Grandpa went to the police station and waited on a bench outside until they opened the station. He went in and turned himself in, was arrested, and sent to prison in Lublin, where he was tried one year later. He was sentenced to eighteen months in a civil prison, but as he had already served twelve months while awaiting his trial, he would serve only the remaining six months. He was released in spring 1941, along with his partners, and they returned to Włodawa. During the time he spent in prison, Aunt Eva and her new husband moved to Lublin (which was Meir's hometown) in order to be near Grandpa and help out. During the time Grandpa spent in prison, they were able to supply him with a small amount of food and clothing. Eva and Meir never came back from Lublin,[10] but Grandpa came home! When he suddenly appeared in Włodawa, he looked a little older, wrinkled, and with his reddish beard greying, but he was the same grandpa, healthy in body, spirit, and mind. He hugged each of us in turn, and then went back to his usual routine.

Life was steadily becoming more dangerous; we never knew what would happen from one day to the next.

Sometime after Grandpa's trial, Uncle Itche was arrested. We never found out what happened to him after he was taken. People just disappeared. They went to work and didn't return, or they were arrested in the street, forced onto a truck, and never seen again.

One evening in spring 1940, we realized that Tata had not returned from work. It is almost impossible to describe how anxious and afraid we all were. The following morning we set about feverishly to find out where he was, but to no avail. Grandpa used his connections and the Judenrat set up an inquiry of its own. It turned out that the Germans had arrested a number of Jewish men on the streets and taken them to work at a place called Belzec.[11] At the time that name meant nothing to us. When days passed and Tata still had not returned, Grandpa, along with the Judenrat, continued in their efforts to have him released. Our worry turned into extreme anguish. Then, two or three weeks later, a miracle occurred: Tata came home. We suddenly heard excited, almost frantic cries, and when we ran outside, there was Tata standing at the gate. But he didn't look like the father we knew. His face was dirty, his clothes tattered and filthy, his eyes lifeless. We ran toward him, but he wouldn't let us near. He went in through the kitchen and asked Mama for a basin of water and some clean clothes, which he took up to the attic. He came back downstairs after quite some time, clean and dressed properly, but was never the same again. And he never told us what he had been through.

The German occupation brought with it many additional changes. In November 1939, many Jews from the city of Kalisz, in western Poland, were resettled in Włodawa. The Jews of Kalisz were expelled shortly after the German occupation, some to Włodawa, others to Plaszów and other places in eastern Poland. Jews also arrived in Włodawa from the town of Mielec, near Krakow. The Judenrat did its best to absorb these refugees into the community. My first boyfriend was one of those refugees from Kalisz—a boy named Mouly Karnovski. The story of Mouly's family is a microcosm of the annihilation of all Polish Jewry.

Peshka, Mouly, and me (left), 1940

His mother came from a well-to-do family in Kalisz. Every summer the family would vacation in Sopot on the Baltic Sea, and there Mouly's mother met a German and fell in love. She left her family, married him, and moved with him to Germany, where they had two sons. Her German husband subsequently died and she married Karnovski, a Polish Jew who was living in Germany. They also had two sons, Mouly and his brother.

One night in 1938, Hitler expelled tens of thousands of Polish Jews and sent them to Poland. Among them were Mouly and his family: his mother, father, and brother (his half-brothers remained in Germany).[12] The family went to live with the mother's father in Kalisz, and afterward, except for Mouly, they moved to Lodź and were trapped there when the Lodź Ghetto was closed. Mouly himself arrived in Włodawa.

Włodawa did not have a closed ghetto as the bigger cities did, but at a certain point, the Germans decided to concentrate all the Jews into one area, choosing a section of streets in the town center that would serve as a Jewish quarter. On January 17, 1941, all the Jews living in Włodawa were ordered to move into that area. We had to leave the compound and courtyard where we had lived our entire lives and moved in with a family acquaintance, Moshe Mandel. The Mandels were fairly well-to-do and had a spacious house in the new ghetto. We were given the use of two rooms, and seven of us settled in: Mama and Tata, Grandma Khaya-Itta, my sisters, Yossl Weller, and me. From our old house we took only the wardrobe, the dining room cabinet, a few personal items, and Grandma Khaya-Itta's treasure chest. Grandpa Shaya, Grandma Rivka, and Itche's wife, Khaya-Sara, moved in with another family in the ghetto.

As memorable as the move to the ghetto was, there is one more event I will never forget as long as I live.

One day, during our lunch break at Antoniewicz's plant nursery, my good friend Peska and I were sitting on the ground eating our meager meal. Suddenly two pairs of black boots appeared in the shrubbery near us. My heart skipped a beat. I looked up very, very slowly, from the boots to the uniforms, and all the way up to the caps

53

against a blue sky, and then quickly looked down. They were two German officers, apparently from the nearby camp. We were paralyzed. A long time passed with us sitting in that threatening silence. Finally, one of them addressed us in German, his attitude business-like, but with a touch of compassion, *"Mensch, du hast keine Zukunft* [Man, you have no future]." And with that, they were gone. We sighed in relief.

---

1. Greenhouse was a forty-year-old bachelor from a wealthy family. He was short and opinionated. His family owned businesses in Gdansk, on the coast of the Baltic Sea, and he managed them. He would visit Włodawa from time to time; when war broke out, he returned for good.

2. Richard Nitschke arrived in Włodawa in December 1939, accompanied by an entourage of S.D. stormtroopers. He dismantled the Polish Municipality and became the sole commander.

3. The street was named after Jozef Pilsudski, a Polish statesman and army commander who served as Chief of State and First Marshall of Poland during the years 1919–27, and instituted a military dictatorship.

4. One brother went to the Soviet Union. A sister (Sonia Kornfeld) had already been living in Brazil since before the war. Their mother remained in Warsaw with two of her daughters, while their other children were sent to stay with relatives.

5. After the war, telegrams were found that had been sent by Shmuel Weller, Yossl's father, in his search of his son. Of all the family members in Europe, none survived the war. In 1946 Weller sent an affidavit for me and my husband to allow us to immigrate to the United States. He was willing to take financial responsibility for us in the United States, but we declined the offer and chose to go to Israel. Weller remarried, and in 1958 he visited us in Israel with his new wife.

6. The Germans instituted a policy of confiscating Jewish businesses and transferring them to "trustees," whom they appointed. They also instituted a policy of forced labor for all Jews between the ages of fourteen and sixty. Finally, they began to systematically rob the Jews of their property.

7. Andje and Sheindele married and had children. Andje remained in Poland after the war, married Ignaz Lichtenberg (Moshe's brother), and emigrated to Israel in the sixties. She died in Hadera in 2011. Sheindele married Yekhiel Greenhouse, and after the war they lived in Venezuela. She died in 2000.

8. The Soviet POWs who joined the Germans were nicknamed Vlasovs, after the Soviet general Andrei Vlasov, who surrendered to the Germans in 1942 and agreed to collaborate with them against the Soviet regime.

9. From German *Gänse*, meaning geese. His real name was Adolf Schwab, He got his nickname because of the way he walked.

10. Much later we received a postcard from Meir, in which he wrote, "Hello, I am feeling fine. I have arrived in a place called Majdanek." That was more or less what he wrote. We assume he perished at the Majdanek concentration camp.

11. Belzec concentration camp was the first of Operation Reinhard for the eradication of Polish Jewry. It was built adjacent to the train track on the Lublin-Lvov line. At first it was a work camp for Jews, but it was converted into an extermination camp in April 1942.

12. The reference here is to the deportation to Zbanszyń) a Polish city near the German border). Between November 1938 and August 1939, tens of thousands of Jews with Polish citizenship living in Germany were driven from there and forced to cross the border into Poland. However, Poland refused to absorb them and the displaced people spent many weeks in Zbąnszyn in the open air. Many died. Only in January 1939 did Poland and Germany reach an agreement and the survivors were allowed into Poland.

5

THE HEART OF DARKNESS

June 1941–April 1943

June 21, 1941. We didn't sleep a wink the whole night. At 3 a.m., my immediate family and the Mandels all climbed up to the roof of the Mandels' house. All the girls were carrying backpacks that Uncle Avremele had brought from the army in which we packed personal items, first aid, and other essentials. As we stood on the roof, we gazed eastward. For the previous few weeks, we had noticed military activity in Włodawa and the vicinity and felt something was going to happen. Then one day, Grandpa came back from work and said Falkenberg had let him in on a secret: the Germans were planning to attack the Soviet Union. This news led to feverish discussions and speculation, particularly on how the war between the two great powers might affect the Jews. Certainly, we thought, a battle of this scope (an Armageddon?) would distract the Germans and they would pay us less attention. Perhaps the Germans wouldn't win so easily. Or maybe they wouldn't win at all. In any case, Tata said we needed to prepare for war.

And so we stood on the roof in the early hours of the morning and looked hopefully towards the east. At dawn we could see the Germans in the distance, building a pontoon bridge across the Bug River. It wasn't long before German forces began to cross to the eastern bank. As the morning wore on, we watched as endless rows of tanks, cannons on trailers, armored vehicles, motorcycles, and troops crossed the river. For three hours we stood and watched as the German army marched into Soviet territory—not a single shot was fired. With heavy hearts we climbed back down.

From that day on, the decrees against the Jews worsened and the atmosphere became increasingly oppressive and threatening. In November 1941, with winter approaching, a new decree was announced that all Jews were to immediately hand over all their furs to the German authorities, and anyone caught hiding them or wearing even a scrap of fur would be executed on the spot. For Jews locked elsewhere inside ghettoes, it was yet another humiliating decree, but for us, it was something else: the first sign that the campaign in Russia was not going as well as the Germans had expected. The Nazis had been certain the campaign would have been won by the end of fall, so they had not outfitted their forces with winter clothing. Now they were in desperate need of even the smallest scrap of fur. As a wealthy family, we had many furs, including some expensive ones. We handed in a few, and the rest we entrusted to a Pole, a blacksmith by trade, who lived near our compound.

In the spring of 1942, a trainload of Jews from Vienna that arrived in Włodawa carrying almost a thousand people meant big changes. There was no ghetto in Vienna; its Jews had been taken from their homes and transported to

Poland in a regular passenger train. They were even permitted to carry suitcases and other pieces of luggage. Upon arriving at the train station in Włodawa, they were instructed to leave all their belongings on the train with the promise their belongings would be delivered to them at their new places of residence. All of us, Jews and Gentiles, were astounded to see these Jews who had not yet experienced hunger, poverty, and persecution and whose faith in the authorities had not wavered. They truly believed they were being resettled and they would see their luggage again. They were dressed elegantly in the latest European fashion, and when it rained they wore colorful transparent nylon raincoats, the likes of which we had never seen. I saw women wearing necklaces with crosses, and I remember one beautiful young woman in a summer dress and cork-heeled sandals.

The Judenrat arranged for all of them to lodge with families in town, ours included. A woman and her twelve-year-old daughter were assigned to stay with us. The daughter, Hildegaard, was depressed. She refused to eat or bathe, while her mother spent her time writing letters and mailing them through the Jewish post office in town. She wrote to Shanghai, China—who would have thought there were Jews in China? She also wrote to a kibbutz in Israel where her eldest daughter lived.

More Jews were transported to Włodawa from other places: some eight hundred from Mielec, near Krakow, and a few hundred more from surrounding villages arrived. The ghetto was becoming extremely crowded. About that time, the Germans recruited a group of Jewish workers and ordered them to dig up the headstones in the Jewish cemetery. Some even had the horrific job of digging up their own families' stones. The headstones were then used to pave a few streets in the center of town, near Solna Street, where the great synagogue was located.

Then came an even more horrific development, an indication that the end was near for Włodawa. Beginning in March 1942, Jewish workers from Włodawa and neighboring villages were ordered to build a camp—fences, shacks, and a few brick buildings—near the village of Sobibor, about eight kilometers south of us. Then, one day in late April, three of the workers (Shamai Triberman, Shmuel Machless, and another fellow named Matiss) suddenly showed up in town, totally naked, telling a gruesome story.

When the camp construction was complete, the Germans gathered the workers and ordered them to get into groups and enter a certain building for a shower. The three survivors could not understand why they saw groups of men enter the building but no one exiting. Since they had been involved in building the camp, they knew the supposed bath house had only one way out. That was why they decided to escape. At the first opportunity, they slipped away, climbed over the fence—which was not yet electrified—and made their way to Włodawa. The Germans immediately issued a warrant for their arrest, and as was their modus operandi, threatened that anyone hiding them would be executed.

The Jews of Włodawa realized the sickening truth: an extermination camp had been erected right outside of town.

At first, many refused to believe it, but there were more and more signs. Poles and Ukrainians from the area reported seeing trains arriving full of people and leaving empty. Rumors spread about gas chambers, and soon we began to see smoke rising on the horizon to the south. We knew full well what was happening.[1]

In May 1942, the roundups for the death camps began in Włodawa. The word for roundup was *Aktzia*, from the German *Aktion*, meaning "operation." As elsewhere, these roundups were given names and numbers. But for those there, no words could express the horror and terror. Nevertheless, for the record, these are the five roundups during which most of the Jews of Włodawa were annihilated.

1. The First: Friday, May 22, 1942 (Shavuot)

2. The Second (Children's Aktzia): Friday, July 24, 1942

3. The Third (The Big Aktzia): Sabbath, October 24, 1942

4. The Fourth: Sabbath, November 7, 1942

5. The Fifth (The Last—*Judenrein* [Free of Jews]): Friday, April 30, 1943.

In May 1942, the Judenrat was ordered to compile a list of all Jews who were incapable of working for reasons of illness, disability, lack of work permits, and so on. On May 22, the Germans announced a decree that all Jews whose names were on the list were required to gather at Zachenta Cinema in town to receive new work assignments. The Jewish police received the list and removed those people from their houses. By evening, approximately fifteen hundred people, including most of the deportees from Vienna, were packed inside the small cinema. It was terribly overcrowded. Then the Germans threw hand grenades into the building and dozens of Jews were killed or wounded. The survivors—some thirteen hundred people—were marched to the train station at Orchówek and from there were transported to Sobibor.

The town was stunned. This most horrific event seemed to prove a connection between having working papers and staying alive. So all who did not have the necessary documents did their best to get them, even by means of bribery, threat, or fraud. We felt fairly secure because we had regular jobs, but what about our parents and Grandma? The cooperative store closed and Khumka and Tata had to return home. Yidiska and I continued to work for Antoniewicz and occasionally worked in his private garden. From there we had a clear view of the wall of the Jewish cemetery, which is how we came to witness the tragic death of the Rabbi of Radzyń.[2]

One day, we noticed some commotion near the entrance of the cemetery. We heard distant sounds of a struggle. There was shouting, with two Germans dragging a third man between them. From a distance of twenty or thirty meters we saw the two S.D. officers—Anton Müller, who was short and thin, and Genze, who was tall, stout, and tottering like a duck—forcibly dragging a tall and stout man: the Rabbi of Radzyń.

The Admor of Radzyń, Rabbi Shmuel Shlomo Leiner, had come to Włodawa at the beginning of the war with his wife and five children from the small village of Radzyń, not far from Włodawa. He was only thirty-three but already had his own following and a reputation as a brilliant scholar. Despite the curfew, Tata would sneak out some evenings after work to hear the rabbi speak about Torah and was deeply impressed. The Rabbi of Radzyń understood early on that the Germans intended to annihilate the Jews and preached rebellion.

Immediately after the first roundup, he declared three days of fasting in memory of the victims. The Germans got wind of it and ordered the Judenrat to arrest the rabbi. Jewish policemen proceeded to jail him in the Jewish prison (normally meant for those who didn't pay their taxes). Moshe Mintz, a young Jewish policeman from a good family, was appointed to guard him. While in jail, the rabbi tried to convince Mintz to let him go and escape to the forests with him, but Mintz refused. He had a wife and small daughter—how could he leave them?

Meanwhile his disciples and the Judenrat did everything they could to get him released. A considerable sum of money was collected and handed over to the S.D., and finally the rabbi was freed and transferred to a German work unit, the *Todt* in Tomaszowka.

A few days later, however, Nitschke ordered him returned to Włodawa. He was then taken by Müller and Genze to the Jewish cemetery. The rabbi put up a struggle, but they pushed him forward, beating and kicking him. At one point they let go of him and he spat at them. When they got close to the gate at the entrance to the cemetery, they stood him up, drew their pistols, and shot him. We heard seven shots. The rabbi fell and the Germans went off.

Yidiska and I ran to ask Antoniewicz whether we could go to town to let people know that the Rabbi of Radzyń was lying dead at the entrance to the synagogue. He gave us permission, but it turned out that Mordechai (Mottle) Reichman, one of the rabbi's followers, had also seen what happened and told the whole story. The rabbi was buried in the cemetery. Sometime afterward, Moshe Mintz was stabbed in the back and seriously injured. He was sent to a hospital in Lublin and returned paralyzed from the waist down, in a wheelchair.[3]

Once, when Yidiska and I were working in Antoniewicz's private garden, we couldn't resist the urge to eat a few unripe green tomatoes. The next day we both started vomiting and had diarrhea. We were sure it was because of the tomatoes, but it turned out we both had abdominal typhus.

I recovered after about two weeks, but Yidiska was sick for much longer, and even when she was over the worst of it, it took her weeks to get her strength back.

For some time, life went more or less back to normal, but then on June 24, 1942, the horrendous Children's Roundup took place. Khumka and I went to work as usual when suddenly the Germans came, stood us in a row, and checked our work permits. In the town, the Germans ordered all those with children under twelve to go with them to the sports field. Most went, but many hid with their children. The Germans and their Ukrainian collaborators (in black uniforms; we called them "Blacks" for that reason) forced them out of their houses. By noon there still were not enough parents and children in the field to the Germans' satisfaction, so the Germans ordered the Judenrat to come with their families. At a certain point, the Germans forcibly separated the children from their parents and threw the children into waiting trucks.

All the witnesses told of shocking and dreadful sights. Many parents went with their children. The most prominent was Rabbi Mendel Morgenstern, chief rabbi of Włodawa. It was said that he and his wife drew lots to determine which of them would go with their young children and he drew the fateful lot. The Germans ordered him to go home, but he refused and went to his death with his children. Lederman's older sister, who worked with us at Antoniewicz's, was hiding with her young daughter along with some other parents and children. Her little girl started to cry, and the other parents, fearing they would all be discovered, told her to leave. Thus, she had no choice and went to the sports field. When Sheindele's husband heard that his wife had been taken, he left his work at Falkenberg's, ran to the field, gave his watch to the Ukrainian guard to let him through, and went with his wife and daughter to Sobibor.

And then, again, life went back to "normal," which meant slave labor, starvation, overcrowding, disease, terror, and fear. The Germans didn't even hide their intentions. The smoke from Sobibor could clearly be seen rising in the horizon. We knew what was in store for us, including many of the details. Yidiska and I talked about it often, trying to imagine what it would be like. We felt that we still had our whole lives to live. It was such a waste—we were so young, barely grown up. What had we even accomplished? We really wanted to live.

Summer was almost over, and autumn was in the air. The nights were colder. It rained more often. Meanwhile the town was again filling up with Jews from all over. They were being transported from small towns and villages in the area, and even from the work camps at Krychów and Osowa in our district. There was absolutely no more room for people in the houses; many of the newcomers simply wandered and slept in the streets. That was the first time we saw Jews dressed in striped uniforms and wearing wooden clogs. They were German-speaking prisoners from a work camp at Bratislava, Slovakia. As conditions became more crowded, it was clear that soon there would be a new—third—roundup.

This time we decided to take precautions. In the Mandels' house there was a cellar. The entrance was through an opening in the floor near the kitchen door. Tata and Moshe Mandel decided that the moment the roundup began, all members of the household would go down into the cellar and hide there, and Tata and Mendel would cover the cellar opening with a heavy wardrobe. The two would then hide somewhere in the house.

Tensions were rising. The evening before the roundup, Falkenberg hinted to his workers that something was going to happen. He didn't say anything explicit, but in passing he happened to mention there had been a terrible roundup in Chelm. When one of his workers asked if he thought there would be one in Włodawa, too, he said, "Maybe." However, he did more than just hint. He also hid many of his workers' families in his house and yard. The night before the roundup, Falkenberg told his workers to get to work at 3 a.m., which signaled to the whole town that the roundup was scheduled for the next day.

From very early that morning, we started to hear shots from the direction of the town. Yidiska was still very weak, so it was decided she wouldn't go to work in order to not risk the "selection." Khumka took her place and the two of us went to work—we assumed those who had work wouldn't be rounded up and taken. The others went down to the cellar. However, when Khumka and I got to work, we were ordered to go to the sports field, stand in line, and wait.

Saturday, October 24, 1942 was a cold and rainy day. It poured in the morning, and throughout the rest of the day there was a fine yet penetrating rain. Mud and puddles filled the roads, and the sports field was soaked. We stood there in our coats and scarves and waited. As time wore on, the field filled up. There were S.D. forces, Ukrainians in black uniforms, gendarmes, Polish policemen, and Jewish policemen. More and more Jews were being brought.

Then it dawned on us. They are rounding up the whole town! With increasing alarm we tried to see if our families were among them. The noise and commotion increased, too. Then we saw all of Falkenberg's workers there, too— all two thousand of them—streaming into the field. Now the picture was totally clear: this was the Big Aktzia, the one that would annihilate the whole Jewish population of the town, workers included. Włodawa would be Judenrein —literally clean of Jews.

By noon, the sports field was practically filled to capacity. People stood in groups. The Jews from the villages stood in one place. The prisoners from Krychòw and Osowa stood together in their tattered striped uniforms, barefoot, all skin and bones, and shivering corpse-like in the rain. Falkenberg's two thousand workers stood in rows—young, relatively healthy and robust, and wearing rubber boots. The Lithuanian and Ukrainian "Blacks" patrolled the field in their police uniforms, looking for any excuse to attack helpless Jews. The S.D. ran about like frenzied locusts. Dogs barked, men and women screamed and sobbed, and here and there shots were heard.

At about two o'clock, Nitschke arrived with his entourage of S.D., and one of them began to read names from a list he took out of his pocket. Those whose names were called were moved from the large field to the tennis court across the street, next to one of the government buildings we knew as the Clerk's House.

There were eighteen men and women chosen—all artisans whose skills were required by the Germans: Lehrer the watchmaker and his wife and daughter; Zilberstein the metalworker; two of the Adler sisters who did embroidery work for the Germans; Moshe Lichtenberg; Yekhiel and Leon Greenhouse; and one glazier, Uncle Avremele. Some of Falkenberg's workers were also added to the group, apparently chosen by him, bringing the total to about fifty. Falkenberg himself was nowhere to be seen.

Then Nitschke and his men left. We were certain we were all going to die. Almost immediately, and with fierce brutality, the Germans started to separate the men from the women. There was screaming, violent beatings, and shooting. Then they tried to separate the women from their children, but the resulting outcry was so great that they gave up. Finally we were marched in two giant rows —men and women. An endless stream of Jews left the sports field in lines of five. My line consisted of myself, Khumka, Peska, and her two older sisters, Bella and Batya. One of the sisters was carrying her baby daughter in her arms, a beautiful two-year-old. Those in the tennis court watched the procession, looking for their families, and when they spotted them they screamed and shouted uncontrollably. As we passed the tennis court, Avremele saw us, shrieked, and held his head in despair. We waved to him and kept walking.

Through the streets of Włodawa, we walked in our rows of five. Guards stood at regular intervals on both sides of the street: S.D. men, Ukrainians in their black uniforms, gendarmes in green, Polish policemen, and even customs workers. Some of the guards held dogs on leashes. Poles watched our procession in silence from their windows and balconies. Suddenly I found myself at the end of the line, in the last row of five.

We reached the town square and witnessed an ungodly commotion. There were hordes of people, including peasants (with their carts or wagons) who had been called up in advance. Corpses were lying around here and there, and wounded were sitting on the ground and bleeding profusely. Lost children were running around crying. And above all that were the Germans, shouting and firing. Near Greenstein's pharmacy stood two Germans. When we passed by, one of them shouted, "*Die Zwei Junge! Komm her*! [You two youngsters! Come here!]" Khumka and I looked at each other in fear and went. The German pointed to two bodies and ordered us to load them on a nearby cart.

I believe that was the first time I had ever seen a dead body. We bent down and tried to lift one of them. We pulled it this way and that, but it was too heavy for us. But a peasant helped us and we were finally able to lift the bodies onto his cart. Then we loaded carts with more bodies, not just of the dead but the wounded, the elderly, the crippled, and the lost children. It was unbearable. I remember one dying man dressed in a striped uniform who suddenly muttered in German, "*Oy meine Schuhe*! [Oy, my shoes!]"

Meanwhile the square was slowly emptying out. Suddenly our job was finished. The procession had moved on, the carts were gone, and the two Germans had disappeared. We were alone. I took off my blood-drenched gloves and threw them away in disgust. Thinking back, I suppose we could have gone home, but the thought never occurred to us. Above all, we were afraid of being alone in that inferno. And what would have been the point of going home anyway? The whole town of Włodawa would soon be "Judenrein." Our brains couldn't function. Our senses were blunted. Without giving it too much thought, we rushed on and soon reached the procession. We pushed through the rows of muddied people and rejoined our row of five.

We soon crossed the bridge over the Bug Canal. From there, the path wound down toward the train station at Orchówek. From the moment we crossed the bridge and left the town behind, the Germans started to push and prod violently. Many Jews slipped and fell in the mud. It was raining harder. The only thing we really thought about was how to continue without falling. Those who fell couldn't get back up. They were either trampled underfoot, torn to shreds by the dogs, or shot by the Germans. Suddenly one of the "Blacks" came up to me and shouted something in Ukrainian: "*Koltzo!*" I didn't understand. Then he pointed to my gold ring and repeated himself. I took off the ring and gave it to him.

We arrived at Orchówek in the late afternoon and were ordered to sit on the embankment by the train tracks. We sat on the muddy ground and waited. I remember Khumka and I debating whether we should eat the sandwich we had brought to work or wait until we got to Sobibor. Would there be time there or were we going to die immediately? I don't remember what we decided. So there we were—eight thousand or more people—sitting on the embankment, and below were the Germans and the others who had led us there.

Sometime later, in the distance, we noticed a commotion as if something were about to happen and saw some people being led away. Little by little, a group of young people, all wearing rubber boots, were assembling on the other side of the Germans. Someone said that Falkenberg had come to get the rubber boots he had given his workers. Then we saw there were also women in the group, and they all had their boots. The group was gradually growing—what was going on?

Khumka and I decided to climb down the embankment toward the front to get a better look. It was a horrifying sight. We saw Falkenberg standing to one side across from his workers and choosing from among them. The workers were standing in a mass, waving their work permits and shouting, "*Herr Chef!*", hoping he would choose them. The Germans pushed them back with their clubs and rifles. Many were already wounded and bleeding. Elsewhere we saw Jews that had been sitting on the embankment now trying to push their way into the group Falkenberg had chosen and the Germans beating them back, shooting them, or setting their dogs on them. A few Ukrainians struck one woman sprawled in the mud with the butts of their rifles. Should we try to get into the chosen group, too? We were scared to death, and besides, we didn't work for Falkenberg.

While we were pushing our way forward and wondering what to do, we saw the Gurfinkels: Irena, Marissa, and Shimek, and the beautiful Nekhama and her infant son, and also my good friend Fella. The reunion was very touching—we hadn't seen them since we left our compound! To this day I wonder how it was that the Gurfinkels were taken in the Big Aktzia. They had so many connections with Poles and didn't look Jewish. They could have gone into hiding with one of their many friends.

Suddenly, one of the *Schutzpolizei*, or *Schupo* for short[4]—the German police in green uniforms and caps—started a conversation with Khumka. It turned out that he recognized her because he used to go into the cooperative store on cold days when on guard duty at the market. "What are you doing here?" he asked Khumka. "You need to be over there." He pointed to the group of workers that Falkenberg had assembled. Khumka didn't move. She pointed to me and begged in despair," *Meine Schwester auch bitte, bitte.* [My sister too, please, please]."

"Okay, your sister, too," he said. "Run."

Khumka started running, with me close behind. She had almost gotten past the Germans when suddenly one of them blocked my way and shouted, "*Zurück!* [Go back!]" I was about to turn back. Khumka stopped in her tracks, not knowing what to do. Then the Schupo suddenly reappeared, grabbed me by the elbow, and led me to Falkenberg's group.

A short while later, Irena, Marissa, and Fella joined the group, too. We were standing next to two sisters, Pessia and Tamar, who worked for Falkenberg. Both were covered in blood and feared that if they seemed injured, they would be turned away. They asked me to stand in front of them in the first row. I refused, but eventually found myself where they wanted me.

Meanwhile Falkenberg had finished selecting his workers, but when he scanned the group, he immediately saw that it was too big and that there were many "infiltrators." We later learned that he had received special permission from

Lublin[5] to take four hundred of his workers. At this point, he began to repeat the whole selection process. He passed through the rows, and if he saw a face he didn't know, the person was sent back. As he came nearer, we knew we weren't safe. Irena, Marissa, and Fella were standing not far from us and were sent back. All of a sudden, Falkenberg stopped, waved his hand in disgust, and said, "Enough."

The selection had ended.

We walked back to town almost at a trot—the whole group that Falkenberg had chosen along with some others. We were pretty sure there wouldn't be any Jews left in town since the roundup had been so total. But when we crossed the Bug Canal and got closer to the ghetto, I suddenly saw Yidiska running toward me. Jews had left their hiding places and were lining the street, hoping that some of their loved ones would be returning. And Tata and Mama were there, too. It is almost impossible to describe our tears of joy and relief. It was almost impossible to bear. I went up the stairs and glanced at the neighboring houses. The doors were wide open, and the houses had been plundered and abandoned. There were dead bodies in the streets. I can't let go of what was racing through my mind: am I dreaming or is this real? The town was almost empty. Ten thousand Jews had been murdered, yet here I was surrounded by my family. And then Mouly Karnovski came, too. That was the first time he had ever dared to visit us at home. To celebrate the occasion, Tata opened the bottle of expensive liqueur he had been saving for his oldest daughter's wedding. We had a toast and then ate, bathed, and told everyone what we had been through. And we all went to bed. Was it a dream or reality? The sensation remained.

The Big Aktzia was over. Aside from the four hundred workers that Falkenberg had chosen and one hundred others, there were hardly any Jews left in town. Falkenberg had received permission to build a work camp in the town for his laborers, and soon a wooden fence was erected that enclosed a number of streets in the existing ghetto. All the workers started to move into the camp. Other Jews did their best to obtain entrance permits to the camp. Grandpa Shaya had a good relationship with Falkenberg, so he managed to get permits for the whole family except for Yossl Weller, who was not registered with the town authorities, and Grandma Khaya-Itta. We were allotted a tiny two-room apartment in the camp and got ready to move. Yossl decided to leave the town the first chance he got and head for Adampol—a place that would soon play an important part in the story of Włodawa's Jews. We found a place for Grandma Itta with some other elderly people in the ghetto, and after dark I would sometimes bring her food.

The situation was now totally transformed. We knew we were going to be annihilated and that even workers were not immune. But those who worked had more time. Tata started to prepare us as best as he could for what lie ahead. His main goal was that there would be a survivor among our family. Thus, he would lecture us every evening after dinner, "Save yourselves. There is no point in dying for someone else whom you cannot help anyway." Again and again he emphasized, "Life is a central tenet of Judaism." He would quote the Bible, "I have set before you life and death, blessing and curse.

Therefore *choose life*, that you and your offspring may live."[6]

For each of us girls, he prepared a strip of cloth on which he had written three names and addresses. In case any of us survived, we should contact them: Uncle Weller in New York, relatives in Palestine, and Schneiderman in Venezuela.[7]

After the Big Aktzia, Tata decided not to sell Grandma Khaya-Itta's valuable religious articles but to bury the whole chest to save for an emergency. He wrapped the valuables well and repacked them in a smaller wooden box that he nailed shut. He buried the box in a small shed in the yard. He then gathered all of us and said that whoever survived the war should come back for the box and use the items. There was also a long strand of pearls belonging to Grandma that he stored in a bottle and buried elsewhere.

Tata understood what was happening in the early stages of the Holocaust. He had an uncanny ability to predict what would happen—that Hitler would be defeated, and even that Israel would become a state. However, when he started to give his clothing away to the needy and we asked him why, he said, "I won't need them. Anyway, I will be the first to go."

* * *

In 1945, after the liberation, I returned to Włodawa with my husband, Misha. One day, we went to the house that had belonged to the Mandels. We found it, and after explaining the story, asked the Polish owner if we could dig in the shed. She agreed and even gave us a shovel. The floor of the shed was covered with potatoes, which we packed into baskets and put outside. Then Misha started digging, and eventually a shovel hit a hard surface. Misha continued digging furiously and finally uncovered the wooden box exactly as I had remembered it. With expectation and excitement we pried the top open. It was empty.[8]

* * *

Between October and November 1942, our lives changed again. Bit by bit, people were moving into the work camp. We had moved some of our belongings to the new place, and Yidiska, Yossl, and I were sleeping there in order to watch over the place and our belongings. The rest of the family were still living at the Mandels'. Khumka became extremely depressed and Mama had to take care of her. In the evenings we would all gather at the Mandels' for supper and then return to the work camp before the curfew. My memories of work during that time are blurry. I believe we worked mainly for Antoniewicz, but at least some days we worked for Falkenberg—I have a vague memory of pushing a heavy wheelbarrow along a narrow wooden pathway. Grandpa Shaya, Grandma Rivka, and their daughter-in-law, Khaya-Sara, were supposed to have moved into the camp but had not yet moved their things there. The work permits were checked at roll call every morning and evening, before and after work, but after work, people were free to return to their homes in the ghetto.

Things continued that way for about two weeks. Then one morning, we woke up and saw the camp was closed! Ukrainian "black" guards had encircled the camp. No one came in, no one went out! From inside, we heard shooting and screaming from the ghetto. Only two weeks after the Big Aktzia, a new roundup had begun: it was November 6, 1942.

Inside the camp, all the workers were assembled for morning roll call. While Yossl hid inside, Yidiska and I joined the others at the central square. We stood in formation, and Falkenberg along with two S.D. men checked our work permits. Then one of the Germans stood before the group and announced new regulations. From now on, the camp would be completely closed. Ukrainian policemen would take the laborers to and from work. Anyone leaving the camp without permission would be shot. Anyone caught hiding an "unauthorized" person would be shot, along with all the tenants of the apartment. The list went on and on.

When at last the speech ended, the German stood for another moment. He then pointed to a worker in the front row, a handsome young man named Pavel Szkad from Kalisz, and ordered him to come forward and turn around. Pavel came forward and faced us, and then the German pulled out his pistol and shot him in the back of his head. "That, as you can see, is what will happen to anyone who breaks the rules!" the German said.

As soon as the two Germans had gone, Yidiska and I ran up to the attic of one of the buildings overlooking the fence. From there we had a clear view of what was happening outside. Again, we witnessed the same horrific sights of the roundups: Germans, "Blacks," and policemen were forcibly pulling people out of the houses. Again, the same shooting and screaming. We saw a Jewish policeman we knew and shouted to him, "Moishele, has anyone from our family been taken?" He just looked up at us and gestured helplessly. Later we saw another Jewish policeman we knew and asked him the same question. "Which family?" he asked.

"Chervonogura and Lustigman," we answered.

The man nodded. "Yes, Lustigman has been taken," he said.

We looked at each other in terror. To me it felt like I had been hit over the head with a hammer. No tears came. Tata was gone. What would happen to Mama and Khumka? If Moshe Mandel was gone, too, then the others were trapped in the cellar. And we were not allowed out of the camp. It was an impossible situation. Mama and Khumka were probably stuck below ground, the heavy wardrobe covering the cellar door. Even though they could have entered the camp with their work permits, it was too late, and for us there was no way out. "They will die of starvation," said Yidiska. "That is worse than Sobibor."

The roundup went on for three days. We waited and worried. The following night we could wait no longer. We crept out of the camp—I don't recall exactly how, maybe through a crack in the fence or somehow through the gate —and made our way to the Mandels' house. Walking softly and cautiously in the dark alongside the walls, we reached the house. The front door was wide open, and inside the silence was deathly. The dead body of our neighbor, the shoemaker, lay on the steps. It then occurred to me that our footsteps must sound threatening. I crouched down next to the wardrobe and whispered, "It's us, Yidiska and Surele. We came to get you out."

The wardrobe was heavy, but pushing it inch by inch, we were able to move it. Finally, we could open the cellar door. Mama, Khumka, and the Mandels came out, starved, exhausted, and frightened.

"You need to come back to the camp with us now," we told Mama and Khumka.

"What about Tata?" Mama asked.

"Later. We don't have time now. We have to get back."

We left the Mandels' and again walked quietly alongside the walls and through the ghetto streets until we were back inside the work camp.

At roll call the next morning, to our utter amazement and surprise, in walked Falkenberg with Grandpa Shaya. Grandpa later told us what had happened. As mentioned earlier, Grandpa had been living in the ghetto with Grandma Rivka and their daughter-in-law Khaya-Sara—Uncle Itche's wife. Grandma was elderly and weak and Khaya-Sara had come down with typhus. Grandpa cared for both of them and, on November 6, when the three were forced out of the house and led to the square, Grandpa held on to them and walked with one on each arm. There was a German behind them holding a dog on a leash. Suddenly Grandpa let go of Grandma and Khaya-Sara and made a run for it. The German shot—and missed—and then unleashed the dog. Grandpa kept running with the dog chasing close behind. Suddenly the dog jumped and its jaws closed hard on Grandpa's jacket. In a swift move Grandpa let the jacket slip off while the dog held fast to it and got away. He hid until evening at the house of our former Polish neighbors in the compound, the Mitches'. At night he sneaked into Falkenberg's house across the street, hid there until morning, and came with him to roll call in the morning.

That same evening, Yossl said goodbye and left for Adampol. Yidiska was inconsolable. Mama kept asking about Tata until Grandpa finally told her the truth. He was dead. The only family members left were Grandpa, Mama, Yidiska, Khumka, Uncle Avremele, and me.

That November marked the beginning of the fourth winter of the war.

* * *

Ghetto life resumed after the fourth roundup, but the ghetto itself was diminished and closed off: one street was half in the ghetto and half in the work camp, which was enclosed by barbed wire.[9]

Its inhabitants were Jews who had been in hiding and had survived the roundups, as well as others who had been hiding in surrounding villages or forests and had returned to town with the onset of winter. The Germans did not harm them. Members of the Judenrat were eliminated in the last roundup and the Jewish police force was disbanded. Some of the former Jewish policemen came to the work camp and the others disappeared.

The Germans needed a new go-between, and they appointed Mouly for the job. Mouly had been working for the Germans, and due to his connections he had been spared thus far. He spoke fluent German, so he became a one-man Judenrat. His position also enabled him to enter and exit the ghetto and work camp freely, and he would visit us fairly often. Of Mouly's whole family, only one aunt (Lily) and her eight-year-old daughter (Mirka Bram) remained.

About five hundred people lived in the work camp: there were those whom Falkenberg had chosen during the Big Aktzia, a few more workers and their families who had hidden in his yard, others like Khumka and me who had managed to "infiltrate" during the Big Aktzia, and others who had managed to get work permits one way or another. For the most part, those at the work camp were young people, although there were two "over sixties"— Grandpa Shaya and Benny Bernholtz.

Our days started with roll call and checking our work permits. Then we went to our assigned jobs. Most of Falkenberg's crew continued to work at draining the swamps or felling trees for wood in winter. Ukrainian policemen guarded us on our way to and from work, and they also guarded the gate and the fence. Grandpa and Uncle Avremele still worked for Falkenberg. Grandpa worked in the yard and Avremele worked in the vegetable greenhouse. The three of us sisters worked in Antoniewicz's garden, and Mama worked in his tool shed cleaning goose feathers for use in bedding.

By this time we no longer had any extra sources of food and lived on what we got from the camp authorities in exchange for our work—some bread, rotted or frozen potatoes, and on occasion, horse meat, which we didn't eat since it wasn't kosher. Sometimes Grandpa would manage to sell an item from Eva's dowry, but most of the time we were much hungrier than before. Once I found a jar of jam in our cellar—a real treasure! I would go down there sometimes and lick some jam. Conditions in the camp were vile. The houses were small and overcrowded (the camp was in the poorest part of town), and the outdoor toilets overflowed. The whole camp was neglected, filthy, and putrid.

Camp conditions of cold, starvation, poor sanitation, and overcrowding led to increased disease. One day, Yidiska came down with typhus. She stayed inside and we kept her condition a secret—we didn't want it known that someone in the camp had a highly contagious disease. The disease usually lasts for a week or two and the main symptoms are high fever and a rash. Yidiska started to recover and I thought to myself that if I caught a bad cold, I would avoid catching typhus. So I walked around barefoot in the snow for what seemed like a long time. The next morning I did wake up sick—with typhus.

Now it was my turn to lay ill in bed while the others went to work. I lay there for a few days, half in a stupor and in pain, until I was over the worst of it. One day, I opened my eyes and there was Mouly sitting by my side. It turned out he had taken care of me all through my illness, and as I was getting better he would visit and bring me candies, lemons, and other delicacies.

And so, life as we knew it went on: work, hunger, disease, cold. It was the familiar routine. It went on like this for six months. The routine was clouded over by the deep-felt knowledge that it could end at any moment. Life was temporary. The real cloud—the never-ending smoke from Sobibor—was a constant reminder that a new and final roundup could take place anytime. With this understanding foremost in our minds, we began to prepare for the worst. Experience had taught us that the roundup would come as a surprise, very early in the morning, so every night we folded our clothes neatly, ready to dress quickly in case of emergency. Also, in preparation, many young people built sophisticated underground emergency hideouts, which they called bunkers. These bunkers were built throughout the ghetto and work camp.

A group of men, including Yekhezkel (Khezkel) Huberman and his younger brother Bollek[10] and other friends of ours (mine and Yidiska's), organized to build a bunker. They considered building it under the house we lived in, but in the end they decided to build it at the Ledermans' house. The sisters Sheindele and Esther Lederman were living in their original house on Blotna Street, where they had lived before the war. The entrance to the bunker would be right in front of the wood-burning stove in the kitchen. In those days, all the houses in our area had wood-burning stoves with chimneys. To prevent falling embers from causing a fire, a sheet of tin was placed on the floor in front of the stove, and on it the logs were piled. The fellows worked on the bunker for months after work and at night.

Fortunately, the guards were lax. Aside from morning roll call and Ukrainian police watching the gate, we were left on our own at night and on days off. Thus, the diggers were able to work undisturbed, although quite a lot of resourcefulness was needed to overcome technical difficulties such as getting tools, building supplies, and getting rid of the earth that had been dug up. Finally the bunker was ready: a rather small opening had been dug under the sheet of tin, and from there a wooden ladder led down to a square room with benches and shelves all around. Two buckets of water were always present as well as some bread and other basic supplies for emergency. The bunker had a double ceiling to stifle the echo of footsteps and to make it harder for dogs to sniff us out. Our bunker had room for ten or fifteen people: there were similar bunkers throughout the camp and the ghetto. We all knew where our bunkers were and were trained and ready to reach it at all cost in case of a roundup. Grandpa and Avremele were in a different group, and if needed, we could also go to their bunker.

Despite all our hardships, and despite the certainty of death, we lived our life to the fullest. We were young and wanted to make the most of our short lives. Nothing stood in our way. We met wherever we could, talked, laughed, and sang. We fell in love and broke up. We were the best of friends. Mouly came over nearly every day. He brought a newspaper in German, and he and Grandpa would pore over it, trying to read between the lines and sort out the truth from the lies and propaganda. Afterward, Mouly and I would go outside and sit on a bench behind the house. We talked till late and kissed goodnight. He was an optimistic fellow, funny and almost naïve. Our friendship deepened into love.

One day, Mama caught us kissing and got very upset. She asked me afterward what I was thinking and whether I wanted to marry him. "Marry?" I asked. "Is that what's bothering you? Who knows if we'll be alive tomorrow?"

Even more wondrous was a New Year's party on January 1, 1943. The Ledermans' cousin, Yankele, had come by the previous day and told Yidiska and me in strict confidence that he would be back to take us out of the camp. Why? Where? He wouldn't say. As promised, he came by the next day and Yidiska and I went with him. He must have bribed a Ukrainian guard for we all left without a hitch and went to David Tzinn's house in the ghetto. What a surprise! It was an amazing New Year's Eve party, with food we hadn't seen since before the war, with music and with vodka pouring like water. Most of the others were older than me. They were Yidiska's age. We toasted the new year, ate our fill, danced and sang, and had a great time. Before midnight, Simkha Cohen sang a song he had written and composed himself about Sobibor, which brought us to tears. At midnight, we kissed and then went on dancing.

The party had just started when there was a knock at the door. The Ukrainian guard at the ghetto had come to see what the noise was. He was ushered in, given a seat of honor at the table, and offered glass after glass of vodka, which he drank until he passed out.

It was all strange, almost surreal. And it was my first real party. When it ended, we stood and sang *Hatikvah* (The Hope, which would become Israel's national anthem) and went back to the camp. A New Year? It felt more like a farewell to life.

Winter with its harsh hold on us, was slowly relenting and turning into spring. It was around then that we started to hear rumors of Russian partisans organizing in the surrounding forests. We didn't place much hope in them as it was said they were robbers, murderers, and rapists. But Jews from the villages who had come to the ghetto for the winter told of a group of Jewish partisans under the command of Yekhiel (Khiel) Greenspan,[11] which had organized in the Parczew Forest west of Włodawa. We heard they had weapons and were fighting the Germans and saving Jews. That news gave us hope. But how could we reach those partisans?

In the latter part of the winter, another group of Jewish partisans was being organized by Moshe Lichtenberg, whom we knew from the compound. The Lichtenbergs were well-to-do lumber tradesmen. Moshe had studied at the "Ort" school, which was a technical Hebrew high school in Brest, and worked with his brother in the family lumber business. When war broke out, he wasn't drafted for technical reasons, so in 1939, at twenty-five, he was married to Manya Gurfinkel and a young father. I remembered that Moshe would visit Manya at the compound and as a young girl I was always interested in what the adults were doing.

Moshe Lichtenberg and his wife

Moshe Lichtenberg's father, Shiye, was in the Judenrat and Moshe himself was on the S.D.'s list of essential workers. Although he survived, his wife Manya and baby son and the rest of his family perished in the fourth roundup, which included the Judenrat. At that point, Moshe was totally alone and childless, and consumed with desire for revenge. He left his work for the S.D. and escaped from Włodawa to Adampol and started to organize his group of partisans.

To start, Moshe turned to young Jewish army veterans and those from the villages with means or useful connections. Within a short time, he had gathered a group of loyal followers: Mottl Rosenberg (his second in command), Haim Fishman ("Tanzer"), his radio operator Yankele Lederman, Moshe Lamdan, Israel Fishman, Illka Bornstein, the three Abarbanel brothers from the village of Wytyczno, and two Jewish Red Army soldiers who had escaped from a POW camp, Leon Nemzer and Misha Feldman. After the fourth roundup, the group found shelter in a forest whose Polish ranger, Pepinski, allowed them to stay there. They called the place "the Base." They started to acquire weapons, resorting to underhanded means for acquiring funds. They also recruited new members and reorganized. Moshe himself would show up at Włodawa from time to time, disguised as a Pole (with a mustache he had grown) or a peddler with a cart, and even once as a landowner traveling in a carriage. He met with his friends at David Tzinn's house in the ghetto and in other places.

I found out about all that later from Moshe Lichtenberg himself. At the time he wanted to recruit Mouly, who told me everything in strictest confidence. Mouly was fluent in German and could pass for a German. His position also would have enabled him almost unlimited freedom of movement and access to invaluable information. He told the partisans he would join only if I came too, but they said that for the time being they needed fighters only—they all had wives, sisters, mothers and girlfriends, but

86

they were still not equipped to absorb women. Mouly declined the offer.

Communication was sporadic. From time to time, we would get news from Yossl Weller in Adampol. Messages would come via people who passed through Włodawa, either verbally or on wrinkled scraps of paper. Thus Yossl learned that Yidiska had come down with typhus and decided to visit her. One night, a small group of fellows left Adampol on their way to Włodawa. On the way, near one of the villages, they were surprised by a German ambush. We heard details from the only survivor who managed to get to Włodawa. The Germans opened fire and the group scattered, but they were killed one by one. Yossl was hit while trying to climb over a wooden fence. He fell dead, still holding on to the wooden plank. We told Yidiska only after she had recovered. She grieved for a long time.

It was April and spring was in full bloom. Antoniewicz went to Warsaw on business, and when he returned a few days later, he spoke to the three of us and Mama in the tool shed where Mama worked.

"I have something important to tell you," he began. "An armed uprising has broken out in the Jewish Ghetto in Warsaw. The Jews are fighting the Germans and the Germans are retaliating with great force, destroying house after house. It's terrible."

We were stupefied by the news, but also proud and even slightly hopeful.

Then Antoniewicz went on. "It seems to me that because the Jews are fighting back, the Germans will intensify their efforts to liquidate all the ghettoes still in existence," he said. "This means that time is running out." Finally he added in a rather mysterious tone, "I have an idea, but I have to check it out."

A few days afterward, Antoniewicz met with us again. What he told us hit like a bombshell. "I have been thinking for a long time about how to save one of you," he said. "Recently I heard that some people I know are looking for help on their farm."

He turned to address Mama. "I suggest, Pani Lustigmanova, that I take one of your daughters there," he said. "She would have to pass as a Polish Christian. My wife and I will teach her how to behave like a Christian. I will naturally arrange all the documents."

Then Antoniewicz added one more condition. He wouldn't choose which daughter would go and Mama would have to decide.

We listened in silence. We were silent after he finished speaking and said not a word all the way to the camp that evening. Privately, his idea struck a nerve within me. It was the same dormant hope that we all had, that somehow, by miracle, we would be saved. Was it possible? Would one of us survive by passing as a Christian? We didn't talk about it, but I believe Mama went to ask Grandpa for advice.

The next day, Mama told Antoniewicz that she had decided not to choose. He would need to choose which of her girls would go.

Antoniewicz chose me. Why me? I suppose it was because I was of fairer skin than my sisters and had blue eyes. I also looked more robust than the two of them. Yidiska was in mourning and had just recovered from typhus, and

Khumka looked sad and downcast from depression. Antoniewicz told me to prepare a photo for the document and to pack a few personal items. We would then make arrangements and go.

The next few days were tense with anticipation. I told Mouly about Antoniewicz's offer, and he decided that after I left he would join the partisans. Meanwhile the whole ghetto had heard about the Warsaw Ghetto uprising. The news sent waves of pride and hope throughout.

Meanwhile Mama recited her message to me again and again, "*Mein Kind* [my child], if you survive, don't forget you are Jewish. When it's all over—and it will end one day —go back to being Jewish and light Sabbath candles."

One day toward the end of April stands out in my memory. It was a beautiful clear day, and Mouly had invited me to visit his aunt and her daughter in the ghetto. His aunt Lily was twenty-nine years old and her daughter Mirka was eight. Lily's husband had worked as a manager for Falkenberg and been killed in the Big Aktzia. Lily had a new lover—Haim Tzelnik, a twenty-five-year-old who had already joined the partisans.[12]

For the visit, I looked through the clothes that had belonged to Eva and found a lovely floral print dress to wear that was just my size. It was light and airy with a touch of blue. I was seventeen, my skin was tanned from working at the plant nursery, and I felt young, pretty, and in love, like a bride about to be presented to the family for the first time.

As we walked through the gate and along the only street of the ghetto (Wyrykowska Street), people were sitting outside in the warm April sun and looking at us as if we had just come out of a fashion magazine. It was an unreal memory, as if there were no war at all.

A day or two later, the last Aktzia took place. I never saw Mouly again.[13]

And Antoniewicz still had not returned.

---

1. The extermination camp at Sobibor began operations in April 1942. Over 250,000 Jews from the regions of Lvov and Lublin and from other European countries were murdered there. In October 1943, a prisoners' rebellion broke out during which about four hundred prisoners escaped, but only a few dozen survived. The camp closed down soon after.

2. I testified at Nitschke's trial in Hanover, Germany, in August 1964 regarding these events.

3. Moshe Mintz, his wife and daughter were sent to Sobibor in the Children's Aktzia in June 1942. He was ordered to arrive at the meeting point with his family, along with the Judenrat. Then the Judenrat members were sent back home, but he and his family were sent to their deaths.

4. *Schutzpolizei,* the state protection police of Germany, was a branch of the uniformed police force.

5. According to other testimony, Falkenberg was assisted by another influential German named Holzheimer, who arrived in Włodawa on the day of the roundup.

6. Deuteronomy 30:19.

7. Schneiderman was an acquaintance of my father's. He emigrated to Venezuela before the war thanks to loans he had received from my father and Greenhouse.

8. A few years ago, many religious articles were put on display at the synagogue in Włodawa, which is now a tourist site. I suspect that at least a few of those articles belonged to my family.

9. After the roundup of November 1942, the S.S. and police chief of the Generalgouvernement, Friedrich Wilhelm Krüger, decided to reestablish a small ghetto in Włodawa and promised its inhabitants would not be harmed. The ghetto operated as a forced labor camp.

10. Yekhezkel and Bollek were the only survivors from their family. Yekhezkel emigrated to Israel, married and had a family, and died in 1995. Bollek lived in Germany and died a few years after his brother.

11. Greenspan (age 24, from Sosnowice) formed a group of Jewish partisans in the forest. He was in contact with the Polish communist underground, received weapons from them, and initiated attacks against German targets.

12. Mirka Bram, the daughter, survived and lives in Israel. Contrary to what I remembered, she said that she and her mother lived in the work camp and not in the ghetto. As children were not permitted to be in the work camp, she hid there, and after the last roundup they both got to Falkenberg's yard and from there to Adampol.

13. I don't know for sure what happened to Mouly. I assume he perished in the last roundup.

6

HUNTED

May–September 1943

The first shots were heard in the early morning of April 30, 1943. We awoke in a panic and hurriedly got dressed. I was the first done, so I ventured outside. There were "Blacks" standing on the street corners. More and more shots were heard and people ran about the streets in a frenzy. Aktzia!

I hurried back inside and urged everyone to get dressed fast. We had to leave. We needed to get either to our bunker at the Ledermans' house on Blotna Street or Grandpa's bunker before the doors were closed. From that moment on, everything happened so quickly. Grandpa and Avremele had disappeared. They must have run to their bunker. We started off for ours—me first, followed by Mama, Yidiska, and Khumka. We ran alongside the buildings, staying in the shadows, and somehow managed to keep from being seen and shot at. I don't remember exactly where we ran—we probably tried to reach Grandpa and Avremele's bunker first, but finding it closed, ran toward the one at the Ledermans' house, built by Yekhezkel Huberman and his brother. In any case, suddenly there was Yekhezkel himself, right in front of us.

"Where have you been?" he asked. "Hurry up! We want to close up."

I will never forget how Yekhezkel endangered himself. What bravery and devotion! Without him, I don't know if we would have gotten to the bunker in time. But we did. Yekhezkel stayed behind for a few moments and scattered feathers from goose down pillows that he had ripped apart to create the impression the place had already been searched and ransacked. We all climbed down through the opening in the floor. The floorboard was closed above us. I looked around in the darkness at the people sitting in total silence on the benches. I counted thirty individuals in a space big enough for ten or fifteen.

We sat there for three days and three nights. The noises from outside were clear: shooting, screaming, dogs barking, soldiers shouting orders, people crying and wailing in a cacophony of languages. Once there were even footsteps on the floor above us; fortunately they passed us by after a while.

The heat was becoming unbearable and we could hardly breathe. Our supply of water quickly ran out. Two buckets had been prepared in advance. In addition, two bricks had been removed from the back wall of the house, close to the ground, to provide an air supply, but still it was stifling inside. We started to remove layers of clothing until we were all sitting in our underwear.

The first day passed and night came. The hours passed so slowly. Everyone seemed to be deep in thought. It seemed everyone felt that we would rather die in the bunker than go to Sobibor if we were caught. No, best to have a few grenades thrown in and be done with it. Here and there some people were whispering. Morning finally came and we were still there, heat struck and scared.

On the second night, Yekhezkel, his brother, and two others, went out to assess the situation. The roundup was still in progress and the streets were full of Germans and "Blacks." The four went out again at night to look for food and, more importantly, water. As they approached the pump on the adjacent street, they could see three dead bodies lying around and suspected the place was a death trap. So they went into the abandoned and looted houses but could find nothing edible. Then in one of the apartments there was a dead woman with her arm in a bucket of water. They took the bucket, ran back to the bunker, and closed the floorboard. It was another day of waiting in the darkness and the stifling heat.

On the third night, we felt we couldn't bear it anymore. Yekhezkel, Bollek, and the two others went out again. They climbed up to the attic and looked down onto the camp. When they returned they said the camp looked deserted and that they had decided to escape to the forest. The news spread like wildfire and people started getting dressed with feverish expectation.

"To the forest? We're coming with you," those in the bunker were saying. The forest was for us a beacon, a shelter, a salvation. The very word was magical, bringing with it hope for a new life.

And so we left. One by one we ventured out into the street and cautiously felt our way toward the camp gate. The street was deserted and silent. The Germans had gone and the Poles had finished their looting. Suddenly we noticed that there were other shadows in the streets. With each passing moment, more and more people were leaving their hiding places and bunkers, filling the streets and moving stealthily forward. It was a truly surrealistic sight: Dozens of shadows moving urgently and silently through an empty town to reach the same goal, the gate. And the gate was wide open!

We ran through the gate and kept on running. Leaving the houses behind us, we reached an open area outside of town. Our group had grown considerably, numbering close to one hundred, all swiftly running along the narrow road that led away from the town and through the fields and woods. Suddenly the sky lit up for a few seconds. A flare lit up somewhere and illuminated the night and alarmed us, but we kept running. Toward morning, when we started to hear the movement of wagons in the distance, we moved off the road and made our way toward the large forest. Finally we found ourselves deep in the forest and collapsed, exhausted. We spent the whole day there.

Amid the frenzy, one other event that day stood out. A woman I didn't know approached me and handed me a packet of photos.

"I believe these belong to you," she said.

I looked at the photos and couldn't believe my eyes. They were all pictures of our family. It turned out that as the woman was leaving the camp, she saw personal items lying near the gate and grabbed some photos from the pile. I can only guess that one of the looters had found Yidiska's album and shook all the photos loose, taking only the empty album.[1]

As evening fell, a few of the fellows said it would be a good idea to go to Adampol, so a small group went to scout the area to see if it was feasible. A few hours later they returned and reported that there were a number of Jews working and surviving there, and no Germans. They recommended we go.

* * *

Adampol was the largest of three small villages to the west of Włodawa (The other two were Leśniczówka and Natalin). Until the outbreak of war, most of their lands belonged to a Polish nobleman, Count Jan Zamoyski. Vestiges of the Middle Ages remained up to the modern era. The count would rent out land to the impoverished peasants, who were semi-vassals. When war broke out, the count left Poland with his family and the Germans expropriated his property and lands and appointed an Austrian named Selinger to oversee the lands and the peasants and ensure that the crops were sent to the Germans. Selinger himself occupied the count's mansion, which was in Adampol.[2]

By the time we reached the Adampol villages, a few hundred Jews who had escaped nearby ghettoes were already living there. They had found shelter in all sorts of places such as barns, sheds, warehouses, and haylofts. Selinger took advantage of them, providing only a meager supply of food in exchange for their work. Jews also bought food and provisions from the peasants, either for money or in exchange for work. In other words, it was like a work camp but without fences or guards.

Forced Labor in Natalin, 1943

When we arrived, we looked for a place to stay. The situation was harsh—the village was filled almost to capacity and many of us could not find work. Moreover, we had left Włodawa with literally the shirts on our backs, while Mama had run away wearing her slippers. We had nothing to sell or barter. Fortunately we were with the Lederman sisters, Esther and Sheindele, and they had the foresight to bring two bolts of fabric left over from their shop.

We also heard that Jews would go back to Włodawa at night and sneak into their houses hoping to find money or something of value that could be traded for food. Yidiska immediately decided she would go back home and suggested I go with her. She thought she might be lucky and find something of value, while she thought I should go see if Antoniewicz had by chance returned with Aryan documents for me to pass as a Polish Christian. I decided not to go, thinking I had better stay with Mama and Khumka. And I was afraid to go back to the town. Yidiska went without me in the end, accompanied by a few others. During the night we were anxious and worried, but in early morning she returned carrying a small bundle of dirty clothes. Totally exhausted, she fell asleep with the bundle of clothes at her side. To our anguish and surprise, we woke up that morning to find the bundle gone. Stolen.

The next day, we left Adampol and went to the village of Natalin—Mama, Yidiska, Khumka and me, along with Yekhezkel, Bollek, their sister, Henia, and the two Lederman sisters. There we found an abandoned house and settled in.

How did we survive? In exchange for some bread, we worked at a brick workshop. Also, sometimes peasants hired us to help in the yard. Whatever food we got was never enough, so we would sell some of the Ledermans' fabric to buy more. The situation was dire and a few days later became even more critical: The bolts of fabric were stolen as well. It was a terrible blow.[3]

At that point, we were truly starving. Due to the lack of vitamins, I had bruises and sores that did not heal. I remember I would get up early and walk through the village to filch cream from the jars of milk the peasants had left outside in the sun. Each jar was covered with a piece of cheesecloth and secured with string. The milk would turn sour and a layer of cream would form on the top. Furthermore, my clothes were in tatters and I was dirty. My shoes were falling apart and I was barefoot most of the time.

Then, as if our situation weren't bad enough, Mama got typhus. We made her a makeshift bed out of some planks of wood and a mattress out of straw, and she lay there burning with fever.

The only solution we could think of was to get to the partisans. It was everyone's dream, but one needed money, weapons, or connections. Yekhiel Greenspan's group would show up some nights to visit their relatives and try to convince them to join up. Moshe Lichtenberg's men were also active in the area but were still only recruiting men with weapons or useful experience. Rumors spread nevertheless, and one day, we heard that Yankele Lederman, the Lederman sisters' cousin, was in Lichtenberg's group and that he had five hundred zloty he wanted to give to his cousins to help them survive.

The trouble was we didn't know how we would find him. We started to wander about the forest paths outside the three villages, looking for partisans. Most often I went with Esther or Sheindele, and Yidiska stayed to take care of Mama. The area was extremely dangerous, but we went anyway. We would walk cautiously on the sides of the path at the very edge of the forest to stay out of sight, and any slight sign of danger would send us fleeing deep into the forest, our hearts beating wildly. In the villages, we struck up conversations with Jews we ran into. We hoped maybe someone knew something about Lichtenberg or his group. Our efforts were all in vain. No one had any information, and we did not find a single partisan.

We kept looking for partisans despite the danger. One day, Esther and I were on a path near the village of Leśniczówka when suddenly someone grabbed my arms from behind, covered my mouth, and started to drag me into the bushes. I fought him off with all my strength, but then I noticed that a burly villager had also grabbed Esther, and she was giving him her watch! How ingenious! I immediately took off my watch—a birthday gift from Grandpa—and gave it to the man who was attacking me.

The two pocketed our watches and ran off. We ran back to the village as fast as we could.

Another time, also with Esther, we were not too far from Natalin when we caught sight of two figures in the distance with what looked like rifles hanging from their shoulders.[4] Our flight instinct kicked in immediately like an inner alarm system, and we each fled into the forest in opposite directions. I ran as fast as I could through the woods until reaching a small opening where I stood panting and out of breath. In the quiet I suddenly heard a rustling of leaves, and a doe walked into the opening and stopped in alarm just in front of me. For one long moment our eyes locked: two huge brown eyes staring at me without blinking. *Yes,* I said without words, *I understand; but don't be afraid. I am a hunted animal, too.* With that, she turned and disappeared in the thick shrubbery.

* * *

Our situation improved somewhat with the arrival of two brothers: Srulik Feferman, aged thirteen, and his eleven-year-old brother. They came from a religious family and their parents had been friends of ours. The two boys had lost their family, so we became their adopted family. Before his death, Srulik's father had told him where he had hidden a small treasure in their house at Włodawa. Srulik went back and recovered it. We could barely believe our eyes when Srulik took coins out of his pockets one by one: old gold coins from Russia, piles of Polish banknotes, and, best of all, a large American gold coin. What a treasure!

We talked it over excitedly and concluded that the money would be used to support all of us, and when the time came, we could use it to get to the partisans. Meanwhile Mama advised that the best way to hide the money was to sew it inside Srulik's clothing. She explained how I should do it and he and I went up to the rafters of one of the barns. Rather shyly, Srulik took off his trousers and waited in his underpants amid the bales of hay. I undid the stitches in the lining of the waistband and slipped each coin in separately, sewing it firmly in the waistband. The large American gold coin I sewed inside the small watch pocket. Fashionable men's trousers at that time each had a special pocket for one's watch. Then I wrapped the Polish banknotes up in a piece of fabric and bound that around his knee. What a relief it was when the job was done and the treasure hidden.

Now at least we had overcome the problem of severe hunger. When needed, Srulik would take a coin or banknote out of his trousers and we would buy food. We ate mostly bread and simple soups. We also had a homemade flatbread made of flour and water. Mama slowly recovered despite having no medicines or doctors. And we continued to search for partisans, but still found not a trace.

Jews and Poles came and went, telling stories and all sorts of news and rumors. One day, the news was about the rest of our family and their fate. They were all dead.

Grandpa Shaya and Uncle Avremele had reached their bunker safely and hid there with others, we were told. Grandpa was a heavy smoker, so he would leave the bunker at night and go up to one of the apartments to smoke. One night he fell asleep on one of the beds, and some Poles who were looting the place found him and told the Germans. The Germans shot him right there, where he had gone to smoke and fallen asleep.

As for Grandma Khaya-Itta, she survived the fourth roundup and continued to live in the same third-floor apartment in the ghetto with some other elderly people. I seem to recall managing to get food to her from the camp. Yidiska and I would often think sadly about Grandma's fate, as all her children were already dead. Tragically, all the Jews in Grandma's apartment were killed in the final Aktzia. We heard the Germans threw the old people out the third-floor windows.

The news on Avremele came from Yekhiel Greenhouse, one of the men in Falkenberg's yard. Avremele managed to reach Falkenberg's yard, and even then the German businessman requested permission to hold on to some of his female workers and a handful of men, claiming they were needed to complete an urgent project. His request was approved, and he chose sixty girls and a few men, whom he housed in a shed in his yard. Avremele was among them. However, a few days later, the Germans came and killed all the men they found, Avremele among them, sparing the girls.

Greenhouse survived by hiding behind a pile of logs. From there he escaped to Adampol and eventually reached Lichtenberg's group of partisans. He had brought a large sum of money that had been hidden in his family's yard, and in exchange for the money he was accepted into the group. As for the sixty girls, the partisans warned Falkenberg that the Germans intended to kill them. Falkenberg let them escape one night and they made it to the villages of Adampol.

* * *

During all that time we had no doubt that the Germans knew that hundreds of Jews were hiding out in Adampol and the neighboring villages and that sooner or later they would get to us. At night, we would leave the village and look for safer places to sleep—in barns, abandoned shacks, and even in the fields. We were consumed with anxiety and constantly listened for the sounds of vehicles approaching. It seemed obvious that they would need trucks to transport all of us to Sobibor. Again we were wrong. The Germans didn't come for us in trucks. They had no intention of sending us to Sobibor.

One evening, some villagers told us they heard that the Germans had arrived and were surrounding the village, and that they would enter the village the next morning at dawn. We immediately put our heads together: where could we hide? We eventually decided on some wheat fields some distance from the village. Fortunately, it was summer and the wheat had grown high. Mama would stay where she was and hide under her bed. At nightfall we each went to the wheat fields and hid on the ground amid the stalks. Srulik and his brother hid with some friends in a wheat field closer to the village.

Morning came. It was clear outside. Suddenly we heard gunshots coming from the village, close by and from afar. Single shots and rapid bursts of fire. And shouting. We lay there in the wheat field, frozen and afraid, our faces pressed into the soil. Time passed. All was quiet, except the rustling of wheat stalks. I turned my head and there, a few paces away, I saw a pair of boots. Time stood still. Then the boots turned and walked away.

Soon we heard fewer and fewer shots, and then someone shouted in Polish: the Germans are gone. You can come out now! My legs were trembling when I got up. Not far from me I saw Yidiska and Khumka and the Lederman sisters standing, safe and sound. We hurried "home" anxiously, and to our great relief we saw that Mama was unharmed. No one had noticed her under the bed boards. Only Srulik and his brother were not accounted for, so we went out to look for them.

What we saw in the village was the aftermath of a massacre. The dead lay everywhere: between the houses, on the fences, in the gardens, and on the streets. We saw none who were wounded and survived. We soon found Srulik sprawled out on his back in the field of wheat where he had been hiding. His brother was standing over him and wailing. Srulik had been shot in the leg, stomach, and head. His leg was drenched in blood from the thigh down. His intestines were exposed through the wound in his stomach and his head had been crushed, brain matter spilling out. I had witnessed death that year, but this was the most appalling sight I have ever seen. The images have remained with me, and they still appear in my nightmares in frightful detail. Almost worst of all, I knew what to do when someone handed me a razor: extract the coins and banknotes from his trousers. How was I even able to do it? I unwrapped the blood-soaked packet of banknotes from around his shattered leg. I cut his trousers and reached to where his exposed intestines were and pulled each coin out. People were standing around and watching in silence. When I pulled the last gold coin out of his watch pocket, someone grabbed it out of my hand and ran off.

We gave all the retrieved money to Srulik's brother and suggested that he should join a group of ultra-Orthodox Jews headed by Mottle Reichman, who were hiding in one of the forests in the area.[5]

Although the Germans were gone for the time being, we knew they would be back. Now that we no longer had all of Srulik's treasure, we couldn't buy food, and our situation was as dire as it had been before. Our sense of urgency grew. We had to find the partisans. The Lederman sisters and I went back to wandering on paths through the forest to look for their cousin Yankele and his comrades.

At last we found them. Sheindele and I went to Adampol one day, and near the entrance to the village was a fellow sitting on the ground at the side of the road. At first glance I thought he looked familiar, and when I took a better look I was sure: Yisrael Fishman! We knew he was in Lichtenberg's group. "Srulke, we've been looking for you!" I exclaimed.

We were so happy that we both hugged him. He gestured with his finger to his lips that we should be quiet, and the three of us moved away so we could talk in private. We described our situation and told him we were looking for Yankele, as he had some money that he wanted to give to his cousins.

"We are not too far from here," Srulke said, "but Yankele is at the 'base' and you won't be able to meet him. I promise to pass on your message."

We stood there and talked for another moment or two. Then, Srulke had second thoughts about his decision.

"You know what... come with me," and he took the path into the forest and started walking briskly.

Srulke led us along paths that twisted and turned through the forest. We walked for two hours or more and reached places we had never seen, but Srulke seemed to know exactly where he was going. We finally reached a large clearing in the forest.

"This is it," said Srulke Fishman, and there before us was an incredible sight. A sheet of tarp had been stretched between some trees. A fire was burning brightly. A few dozen men were standing about or sitting, either cooking or talking among themselves. One was even singing. Here and there we saw weapons, with bandoliers strapped across chests. Finally! My heart swelled with pride. My despair and fear vanished in an instant, replaced by a sense of relief, exhilaration, and freedom. For more than three years I had not felt anything like that.

Immediately we were introduced to Lichtenberg. He looked at me and said, "I know you. You are Sur'ke, aren't you? Chervonogura?"

"I am," I answered.

"What about your family? Any other survivors?"

"Some," I said, and told him what had happened to our family and how desperate our situation was in Adampol.

Lichtenberg took a few banknotes out of his pocket and offered them to me on the spot. Then he asked Sheindele about herself and listened to her story. When he heard her last name was Lederman, he immediately asked her if she was related to Yekhiel Greenhouse.

"He's my second cousin," she answered.

"That is good," said Lichtenberg. "We recently arranged a place for him to hide with a Pole in Potfokule."

His second in command, Mottl Rozenberg, joined in the conversation and the two debated what to do. Apparently Yekhiel Greenhouse had joined their group not too long before, but due to pains in his leg realized that life with the partisans would be too strenuous for him. He asked that a hiding place be found for him in exchange for part of his money. Fairly quickly they found a Polish peasant who agreed to hide him in his isolated farmhouse, for a hefty sum, of course. As part of the whole "bargain," the peasant also sold them a machine gun he happened to own. A machine gun was a heavy weapon for a small group of fighters, but the group was proud to have such a Judgment Day weapon.

Lichtenberg promised Sheindele he would find out whether the same Pole would agree to hide her and her sister. He also promised that Yankele, who was not there but at the base, would find a way to get the money to us. That wasn't all. He said that the group was ready to absorb women and that I would be one of the first. He told us to go back to Adampol and await instructions from him. Meanwhile I should say goodbye to my family, and with the money he gave me I should buy shoes and trousers.

After sunset, another partisan led us back to our village. When we got back, we told the others what we had seen and about Lichtenberg's offer. This was the second time that someone had suggested I leave my family, and the idea was almost too much for me to bear. But Mama gave me her blessing: "*Mein Kind*, save yourself. That's what Tata would have wanted. Who knows, maybe *you'll* be able to save us too."

* * *

A few days later, Lichtenberg's messenger came with the news that the Pole who was hiding Greenhouse was willing to hide only one more person, not two. Esther didn't hesitate. She told Sheindele to go. I said goodbye to Mama, Yidiska, Khumka, and the others. We were all crying and hugging each other and promised to write. I said I would look out for them. Mama had started to recuperate by then, and I felt sure we would all be back together soon. With that, Sheindele and I left with the messenger to the partisans, and from there Sheindele was taken to the farm where Greenhouse was hiding.[6] Not long after, another three women joined Lichtenberg's group: my friend Andje, Yankele Lederman's girlfriend, Khassia, and Khaya Schneiderman. We were four women among about forty, most of them armed.

For the most part, the group was busy getting food and weapons and recruiting members. But they also carried out reprisals against locals who denounced Jews, and even retaliated against Germans. Those actions would always take place at night. During the day we would hide in the forest and do our best to stay hidden and not attract attention. After nightfall we would move on, covering a distance of twenty or even thirty kilometers. Before dawn we would camp down in a new location. We moved about in the woods and fields of the countryside west of Włodawa, sometimes close to town and sometimes far away.

Nighttime was also the time to search for food. Most of our fighters would take part in those activities, and the rest, including those not bearing arms, would stay behind to guard the camp. The partisans would raid villages and isolated farms and at gunpoint steal a pig, a cow, potatoes that peasants had stored in open pits in the fields, flour, or bread. In order not to cause too much animosity, the partisans would pose as Russians.

Water was also a rare commodity. The forest ranger Pepinski, who permitted us to be in the forests under his supervision, also allowed us to draw water from the well in his yard. Each of us carried a bottle, and when we didn't have well water, we would fill it from puddles of rain or from springs or bogs. In order to filter out the silt from the water, we would pour it into the bottle through a piece of fabric. We normally did not have enough water to bathe in—even so we (especially the girls) would sometimes use our drinking water to wash ourselves a little.

Summer was almost over, and the fall weather brought more rain and chilly nights. We each had a blanket to cover ourselves at night. I particularly remember how exhausting it was to make our way on foot, single file, through the dark forests. Those night journeys seemed endless, and I remember marching half asleep, holding on to the belt of the person in front of me and nodding off every time we stopped. I had shoes but still had open, pus-like sores on my feet that didn't heal, which made it hard to walk. We would walk until long before dawn, then set up camp early to avoid running into shepherds, most of whom were young boys. It hadn't taken long for the peasants to figure out that the partisans who had been pilfering their food were not Russians but Jews, and their animosity grew. Therefore, any peasant or herder we might run into was a potential threat. Whenever we reached a new location, I would immediately look for a comfortable tree trunk, wrap myself in my blanket, and sink into a deep sleep. When I opened my eyes in the mornings I would find myself in a new camp site: a clearing in the forest, a fresh green wood, an orchard, a flowery meadow, and once even a pasture full of mushrooms.

Even before dawn, our cook, Knopmacher, would have a fire going and would be cooking. Moshe Knopmacher was a butcher by trade, older than us, tall and stout, a mountain of a man. They said that when the partisans first started out, they would take him on raids in the villages as his hefty appearance would frighten the peasants. But he was a kind and generous man, and he spoiled us girls with special treats. On a few occasions he woke me before the others and gave me delicious hot food he had just prepared. One of his delicacies was baked potatoes in lard. Pepinski also spoiled us girls, and when we passed through his place he treated us to fresh milk, bread, jam, and cheese. There were, however, days when we hardly ate. For example, when we had to move in haste, we had to get rid of all the food we couldn't take with us. We would eat as much as we could and bury the rest.

A nice seventeen-year-old Polish villager, Vladek Kozlovski, was our contact person in Włodawa. He would be sent on various errands in town and would meet with Falkenberg or with the district doctor, Dr. Orzechowski,[7] both of whom aided us. Falkenberg supplied information and sometimes weapons, and the doctor sent essential medications. One day, when Vladek was on an errand in Włodawa, he felt like getting a haircut and a shave. He went to a barbershop in the town center and had his hair cut. No sooner had the barber applied shaving cream when a German soldier came in, his weapon drawn. Vladek was arrested and interrogated. When it was clear that Vladek was late returning, the whole group immediately relocated. With Kozlovski's arrest, our contact with Włodawa was cut off. Shortly after, Dr. Orzechowski was arrested and sent to Buchenwald. Falkenberg was arrested at the same time and sent to Mauthausen, perhaps as a result of Kozlovski's arrest.

Needless to say, there were nightmarish moments, too. Fear came and went in waves but never disappeared, and shattered nerves are not soothed overnight. One such incident that stands out in my mind is not connected to any specific time or place yet plays havoc with my memory. One night, while we were walking through the forest, suddenly I heard shots from the head of the line. We all fell to the ground and waited, but the shots continued. I couldn't stand it anymore. I jumped to my feet and ran as fast as I could through the forest, over bushes, and on a moist carpet of fallen leaves. I ran and ran, not looking in any direction, until I left the forest and found myself in a harvested field. I kept running until I fell down, exhausted, near some trees. I heard moaning and groaning from somewhere and then fell asleep. Morning came and it started to rain, and soon I was lying in a big puddle. The day passed slowly and still I lay there. It kept raining, and my body temperature warmed my waterbed. I felt strangely indifferent, almost at peace with my fate. I could lie there in this warm place and die and be done with it.

The partisans found me in the evening. They carried me a short distance to an abandoned brick workshop where I could hide out until I got better. There was a group of Jews hiding there too, and I remember one woman in particular who told me she knew me—her son had served in the army with Uncle Avremele in Brest. I will never forget the hot soup that woman fed me. It was Krupnik soup, barley and potatoes, and it tasted heavenly.

There were small victories as well, which for us were enormous. One evening, the group went on a raid, and two armed guards and another ten of us stayed at the camp. It was drizzling and we sat under a tarp we had stretched between the trees. Suddenly we heard gunfire —first, single shots, and then a burst of rapid fire. The shots sounded so loud and close that we thought we were under attack. Amid the panic and commotion, I took off again and ran into the forest. I ran as fast and as far as I could until I collapsed, out of breath. My lungs nearly exploded and I felt hopeless and terrified. The forest was pitch black and silent. I didn't know where I was, nor did I know what had happened to the others. I had no idea what to do. Standing there helplessly, I remembered the partisan's password for help. It was a special whistle, something like a bird call, which all the new recruits learned. I whistled, softly at first, and then stronger. I heard a whistle in reply. I whistled again and again the reply came, this time closer. We went on until we were very close. A comrade from the partisans, Yoshe (Yosef) Glintzman, appeared in the dark from behind the trees.

"Do you know what happened?" I asked.

"No idea," he answered.

"Do you know how to get back?"

"Yes. Follow me."

We made our way back to the camp, cautiously and quietly. To our great relief the whole group was there. All our provisions were packed and everyone was ready to move on. They were waiting only for us. While hastily leaving our old camp site, we heard the whole story.

The fighters had gone out to get food, and as was their habit they stopped at Pepinski's, not far from our camp. But when they got close to the forest ranger's house, they noticed a suspicious looking character in the yard. Approaching with caution, they saw that the figure was a half-naked German soldier, washing himself at the well. The partisans burst into the yard, weapons drawn, and ordered the German to surrender, which he did. They then ordered him to lie face down on the ground and shot him. Another German soldier came out at that moment and he, too, was shot. Two more German soldiers, having heard the ruckus, appeared at the window and opened fire, but both were shot and killed. A fifth German, apparently their commander, managed to escape.

Our only casualty was Moniek Bornstein, who was hit in the leg. (Sadly, his wound became infected and he later died.) Our victory exhilarated us. We had engaged in battle with German soldiers and they had surrendered and been killed. Four dead German soldiers—it later turned out they were Hungarians—were lying dead in the yard. Despite a shortage of ammunition, Lichtenberg permitted each of his men to shoot one extra bullet into the enemy soldiers. One by one, each partisan fired a single bullet into the dead bodies and said, "This is for my father... this is for my mother... this is for my sister..."

The group collected what booty there was and returned to the camp. And what precious booty it was! Four brand new rifles, one pistol, ammunition, hand grenades, binoculars, a map (on which Pepinski's forest was marked), boots, coats, and four German uniforms. For the first time we walked through the forest singing. We felt a joyous stupor. We forgot somehow how tired we were. Our aches and pains and hunger were gone, our feet were light, and our spirits high. Revenge was sweet. Our newfound confidence and power engendered a vague and hesitant hope that everything might turn out well in the end.

The sad reality, however, was that our situation was getting harder and more precarious. From time to time the Germans acted to locate and eliminate Jews who were simply in hiding as well as partisans, or "bandits" as they called us. The peasants were becoming more and more hostile, and any passing herder or peasant might notice us and reveal our whereabouts to the Germans. The coming winter didn't make it easier.

At about that time, we were approached by three Russians who had crossed over from east of the Bug River. They proposed that we cross the river and join the Soviet partisans in the east. On the other side of the Bug, they added, the area was completely controlled by the partisans and they were well armed and organized. In addition, the local villagers supported them and paid their crop tax to the partisans, not the Germans. Some suggested we join the partisans at the bogs of Ochoża in the Parczew Forest, where Yekhiel Greenspan's group was. Apparently, they had set up an organized and well-run family camp.[8]

Lichtenberg decided first to check out the possibility of joining Greenspan, and one day, after a long night of walking, we arrived at the bogs of Ochoża. I have two clear memories of our arrival there: first, there was an abundance of water, and after weeks we could finally wash ourselves properly. By that time, there were seven girls in the group and some of them had more clothing, so we could wash our clothes, too. To this day I remember the wonderful feeling of a clean body, clean hair, and clean clothes. Second, there were quite a few Jews among the partisans and families from Włodawa, and each of us found relatives, friends, and acquaintances.

The two groups' leaders, Greenspan and Lichtenberg, met for a long time to discuss unifying their two forces, but the negotiations blew up. It seemed they could not agree on the division of authority between the two commanders. But that proved not the case. One morning, Lichtenberg announced that we were moving east of the Bug. Soon the whole camp at Ochoża had heard the news and a whole wave of partisans and families asked to join. Among them were nine young Jews who had been soldiers in the Red Army and escaped POW camps. There were also older men and women, children, and families. It wasn't long before our group numbered 110. The three Russians who had approached us also recruited a few other Russians; their group numbered six or seven.

Moshe Lichtenberg now accepted almost everyone into the group—all those he thought could cope with the hardships of the journey anyway. He was no longer the angry young man motivated solely by revenge. I like to think I had something to do with the change in him, and I do believe there is nothing like love to soften a person's angry heart.

Moshe and I had a close relationship—and soon were sharing love. During the long days we spent waiting in the forests we would talk a lot. And during our night journeys he would join me at the end of the row and check how I was doing, encouraging me to keep on when I was on the verge of collapse.

"There, do you see how close those trees are on that hill? We're almost there," he would say.

Of course, when we reached those trees we kept going, but that was his way of helping me cope. He gave me a small pistol in a leather holder, "a woman's gun," he called it, and taught me how to use it (only as a last resort, he said, to avoid being captured by the Germans). As for him, he was always well dressed (he came to the forest directly from home, with fine clothing and personal belongings), and carried a pistol and a rifle.

I saw both his sides. On the one hand, he was young, proud, angry, ambitious, and self-confident. He was a natural leader and was able to instil confidence in his followers. On the other hand, he was vulnerable, having lost his wife and child and his whole family. He was looking for warmth, love, and devotion—and he found that with me.

* * *

It was finally time to be on our way. We set out one day, more than one hundred people in a long line, carrying weapons, equipment, and supplies. In total silence we passed through forests and fields and alongside unlit villages. Our Russian guides were supposed to lead us toward a place on the river where guarding was lax and the river was shallow so we could cross the Bug relatively safely. We walked for quite a few nights.

We knew we would eventually make the crossing, but no one told us exactly when. When the order to set out came, it took me by surprise. We still hadn't rescued Mama, Yidiska, and Khumka from Adampol. Yet again Moshe promised me that after we crossed the Bug he would make every effort to save them and send people to bring them east. Their condition was dire. Mama had recovered from her typhus, more or less, but then Khumka got sick, and then Esther. Yidiska took care of all of them. We communicated regularly through messengers, and I still have some of our "letters" written on all sorts of scraps.

We finally reached the river, but then it turned out that the Russian guides couldn't find the place they had chosen for us to cross safely. It was almost dawn and we were still walking. Tempers flared. Our nerves were shaky. When daylight broke, we could see the extent of our calamity. We found ourselves near the village of Slawatycze, close to the river, completely exposed. Across the river we could see the houses of the village of Domaczewo. The forest lay further to the west, and our only protection along the riverbank were low lying shrubs and bushes. This caused an immediate commotion and the commanders lost control of the situation. A few of the Russians announced they were going to the forest and a large group of partisans joined them.

Within minutes Moshe Lichtenberg was left with a decidedly smaller group, a few dozen at most. We had ten rifles (the breakaway group had taken the machine gun) and three Russians who remained with us. We hastily hid in the bushes along the river and stayed there quietly the whole day. The hours passed leisurely. The sun climbed across the sky. In the distance we saw occasional border patrols. Anxiously we awaited nightfall.

The sun set at last and all was dark. People got up, stretched their limbs, and prepared for the coming night action. Two of the Russians took their weapons and said they were going to the nearby village to get food. Without waiting for permission, they left. Soon afterward, gunfire was heard, and the two Russians came running back and shouting, "The Germans are after us! Get ready to fight!" It seemed like a Hollywood film scene. It turned out that the two had encountered German guards and beat a mad retreat under fire.

Now there was no choice.

"We are crossing the Bug here and now," Moshe announced. "There is no time to lose."

We left most of our supplies behind and stepped into the cold water. Fortunately, the river was shallow and the current not too strong. The fighters held their weapons above their heads, and we walked across. Close to the opposite bank, the water was suddenly deeper, but two fellows held on to my arms and carried me ashore. We had almost reached the eastern bank of the Bug when we heard shots at close range, grenades exploding in the water, and flares lighting the sky. The Germans were looking for us, but they just missed. One at a time we climbed onto the riverbank and ran for shelter in the trees.

* * *

The shelter we found was a small wooded area not far from the shore, and we sat there, dried off, and got organized. At daybreak we heard a cart passing just outside the wood. One member of the group went to talk with the villagers and asked where the closest partisans were situated. We quickly learned that the information we had heard about the eastern side of the Bug was true. The villagers didn't bother us and we were able to walk openly during the day! We walked according to the directions we had received, and after a few hours we were stopped by guards just outside a large partisan camp. We had arrived at the Voroshilov *otriad* (an otriad is an independent fighting unit between a company and a small battalion in size). Moshe went to speak to the commander. While we waited for his return, we were getting hungry, so we sent a few fighters to pilfer food from the villagers as we had been used to doing on the other side of the river. For that we were severely reprimanded. Here it was absolutely forbidden to steal from the peasants. There was a central distribution of food organized by the central command of the otriad. Under no circumstances were the locals to be harassed.

Sometime before, I found out that a former Jewish policeman from Sosnovice named Inventash had joined our group. He was the man who had forced my father out of his hiding place during the roundup, causing his death. Inventash linked up with our group somewhere on our way from Ochoża to east of the Bug. Someone pointed him out to me and suggested that I tell Moshe about him. I imagined that Moshe would have tried and executed him, and I didn't want that death on my conscience. The dilemma was terrible, but in the end I decided to say nothing.[9]

The Soviet partisans agreed that we should stay in the forest adjacent to their camp until they decided what to do with us. Meanwhile they included us in their roster for guard duty and made sure we had food. Moshe insisted they let us function as an independent unit, even if under their command, but he also knew that if the rest of our group—those who had separated from us with the machine gun—didn't show up soon, chances were slim that the Russians would agree. With every passing day our concern increased, until finally a team of three was sent back west across the Bug to find the rest of our people and bring them east. Moshe entrusted the three with one more task: to rescue my mother and sisters from Adampol.

The group left at once but returned the next day empty-handed. They said it was impossible to cross the Bug. All the crossing points were heavily guarded by Germans.

Moshe wasn't convinced and sent another team. They, too, returned the next day claiming they had been unable to cross. Moshe was sure they were lying. "I have no choice but to go myself," he said. "If not, we will lose our group and our weapons, and the Soviets won't let us join them."

I burst into tears. I begged and pleaded and tried to convince him not to go. To no avail. He was determined. I had a terrible premonition of danger, but I knew he would not be moved. I also knew this was the last chance to save my mother and sisters.

The time came for him to go. We stood away from the others and embraced. I wept bitterly. He entrusted with me his personal belongings: photos of himself and his family and his gold watch. When we pulled apart and he started to walk away, he turned to me suddenly and said, "Don't worry. I will be back." With that, he was gone.

* * *

Moshe left together with his second in command, Mottl Rozenberg, and with Haim Fishman, the radio operator. Moniek Berglad was appointed to take charge during his absence. Moshe must have asked him to watch over me as well, as Moniek would periodically show up and ask how I was.

The days passed. We camped right outside the Voroshilov otriad base and waited for news. There was a group of about ten Jewish fighters among the Russian partisans, and from time to time they would visit us. Most of them were from Domaczewo. The others were Misha Omelinski from Brest, Moshe Rozes, and two women, Roza and Sonia. They enjoyed being in the company of fellow Jews, and you could tell they quite liked the idea of a Jewish partisan group. I remember going to visit them at the camp with a group of friends and how amazed I was at the sheer numbers of fighters, the abundance of weapons and equipment, their quarters and lodgings, and the well set-up kitchen. It was, in short, a true army base.

The person we had chosen to represent us in our dealings with the Soviets was Siomka (Shimon) Rothenberg. He was fluent in Russian, well educated, and bright. We had heard threatening rumors that the Soviets were about to send us back across the Bug, but so far nothing had been decided. We were told they were waiting for a certain general from the Brest region to arrive and he would decide.

Two weeks passed and one morning, the whole missing group showed up. There were dozens of men and women and even a few children, and even some whom I was sure Moshe would never have accepted. In a long line they entered our camp and were greeted with shouts of joy.

Yekhezkel Huberman was among them, and I was happy and excited to see him. Only three were missing: Moshe, Mottl, and Haim.

"Where is Moshe?" I asked.

"He has a few more things to attend to, but he will be coming soon," someone told me.

I had a feeling something was not right, but it didn't seem possible that everyone would be conspiring to hide something from me. It made no sense. That's what I told myself and I repressed my growing sense of alarm.

It was Yekhezkel who was the bearer of the first tragic news.

"I have to tell you something," he said. "Your mother and Yidiska and Khumka and my sister Henia..." and with tears in his eyes he told me what had happened.

He had stayed in the village of Natalin for six weeks, the whole time trying to persuade his sister Henia to go with him and another friend who promised to lead him to the partisans. But Henia refused to leave without my sisters and Esther Lederman, and the partisans were not prepared to accept five women at once. In the end, Yekhezkel decided to leave on his own for the time being and reached the partisans at Parczew Forest. The next day, Moshe arrived there too, and when he heard Yekhezkel's story he immediately commanded him to go back to Adampol and bring my mother and the other girls back with him. Yekhezkel set out right away and reached Adampol easily. From there he continued to Natalin but found not a single Jew there. Polish villagers told him that only the day before, the Germans had shot and killed all the Jews who had been hiding in the village.

Exhausted and weary, hungry and worn out, his bare feet sore and bruised from walking through the chaff of freshly harvested fields, grief stricken and blind with fury, Yekhezkel made his way back to Parczew Forest. On the way he saw bundles of harvested grain lying in a field and set them on fire. A few days later he crossed the Bug with Lichtenberg's second group.

The two of us sat there and cried. Now I was the only one of my family left alive. My grandparents, parents, aunts, uncles, and sisters were all dead! I was alone in the world. I was the only one left. The sole survivor to carry the memory of my family.

"Yidiska sacrificed herself, and as our father in his wisdom had wished of me, I would carry on their memory," I said to Yekhezkel.

A few days later, the Soviet general arrived in order to decide whether we would go back to Poland, and a meeting was set between our representatives and their officers at a house in the village. In attendance on the Soviet side were the general himself, Voroshilov otriad commanders, and other officers. On our side were Siomka Rothenberg, Moniek Berglad, Khassia, Shmuel Stohl, and me!

Why was I invited? I had no idea then and today I can only guess. I remember with perfect clarity the meeting and much of what was said there. I was seated among all those important officers and commanders, but I was depressed and pensive. I had not gotten over the bitter loss of my mother and sisters and was preoccupied, yet I listened. I already knew some Russian and was able to understand a large part of what they were saying.

The Russians opened by saying that since our group members were Polish, had come from Poland, and have our own country to liberate, why would we need to be in Soviet territory? They repeated their claim and emphasized that we should go back to Poland where the enemy is and fight the enemy there.

Then Rothenberg rose and delivered a long rebuttal speech.

"Comrades, how can you send us back to Poland?" he asked. "We can barely survive there. The partisans there don't have an organized network for support. We don't have enough weapons. Not to mention that your people stole our machine gun and murdered our commander, the person who established our group, and we are sitting in the presence of two who witnessed the murder. After all that, you say you want us to go back to Poland and die there?"

I was stunned. I was suddenly hit by the meaning of what I had heard. The room around me became totally black as if someone had turned off the lights. I shot up and ran out to the yard.

Someone ran after me, apparently Berglad. Murdered? Moshe? How could that be? How was it that no one told me?

I burst into tears. I stood in the yard sobbing uncontrollably. People moved like shadows around me and tried to talk to me, but I heard nothing. Moshe had been killed.

A long time passed before I was able to hear and absorb the whole story. There are several versions of Moshe's death. The one I will tell here is, in my opinion, the true one as it is based on eyewitness reports.

Moshe and his two companions crossed the Bug easily and a few days later reached Ochoża safely, where they found the rest of our group unharmed. Only one item was missing: the machine gun. It turned out that during the skirmish at the Bug, the larger group that had left us did not reach the forest. They, too, had been obliged to hide in the low foliage along the river at some distance from us. When evening fell, they heard shooting and explosions and saw flares in the sky. They assumed that our group had been wiped out by the Germans and the river was guarded too carefully, so there would be no point in trying to cross. The Russian guides claimed that the only reasonable thing to do was to return to Ochoża and reorganize.

The journey back to Ochoża lasted several days. At one of the campsites, two of the Russians (a man named Kulka and one of his friends) approached the two men from our group (Shalom Mirmelstein and Leon Nemzer), who were in charge of the machine gun, and offered to guard it for them so they could get some sleep. Mirmelstein and Nemzer gladly agreed and went to sleep.

When they woke up in the morning, they saw that the Russians had disappeared—with the machine gun. When Moshe heard about the theft, he was outraged and decided to get it back. He asked around and found out that the two Russians would be at a wedding party the next day at the village of Zahajki. He gathered his two companions and two others, Shmuel Stohl and Khassia (Yankele Lederman's girlfriend), and the five of them went to Zahajki. Moshe knew many people in the village, and when the five reached the house where the wedding was taking place, they were welcomed warmly. Suddenly Moshe saw Kulka sitting in a corner with the machine gun.

They exchanged pleasantries, and then Moshe said, "What a handsome weapon you have there. Well done! And where did you get it?"

"I got it where I got it," answered Kulka.

"Maybe you got it in battle. If so, then really well done. But maybe you stole it?"

From then the polite conversation turned nasty and loud, so loud that the host came over and asked them to take their argument outside. "Gentlemen, you are ruining the festivities," he said.

Moshe and his group got up to leave and Kulka followed with the machine gun. It is not clear why Moshe and the others let the Russian follow behind them and why none walked behind Kulka. Maybe they didn't suspect Kulka would run away. Maybe they didn't believe he would dare to harm them during a wedding. Or maybe it was just smugness and overconfidence. In any case, when they walked out the door and into the yard, Kulka opened fire. Moshe Lichtenberg, Mottl Rozenberg and Haim Fishman were killed on the spot. The two others escaped and made it back safely to Ochoża—without the machine gun and without their commander.

---

1. The few photos I have from before the war are the same photos that the woman gave me in the forest on the way to Adampol.
2. Today the mansion at Adampol serves as a sanatorium for tuberculosis patients.

3. We did find out eventually who the thief was. He sold the fabric, bought a weapon, and joined the partisans.

4. Lichtenberg later claimed, based on my description of the event, that the two figures we had seen were him and his deputy, Mottl Rosenberg.

5. Reichman was a follower of the Rabbi of Radzyn. He and the rabbi's brother-in-law and their families dug a shelter in the forest and hid there. Srulik Feferman's brother found their shelter and joined them. One day. Reichman and the brother-in-law went out to buy supplies from local villagers, and when they returned they found the shelter had been discovered and all had been killed. Reichman and the rabbi's brother-in-law survived. Reichman lived in Israel and the brother-in-law went to America.

6. Sheindele suffered a guilty conscience her whole life. Khassia and Yaakov Lederman survived, and after the war they lived in New Jersey.

7. Dr. Orzechowski was a brave and noble Pole and even saved a number of Jews (among them Mirka Bram and Sabena Barnholtz.) He perished at Buchenwald.

8. Family camps were set up near Jewish partisans' units in the forests and sheltered Jewish noncombatants, refugees, survivors, women, children, and older people.

9. Inventash disappeared sometime later. He probably joined a different partisan group. After the war he emigrated to Canada and I heard he was tried for crimes committed during the war but was acquitted for lack of evidence.

7

POLESIA WOODS

September 1943–April 1944

The meeting with the general went well. He decided not to send us back to Poland but eastward, deep into Belorussia, to the Molotov Brigade in the Polesia Forest near Pinsk, southwest of the capital Minsk. There the local command would decide what to do with us. We started to prepare to leave.

The Soviets would not permit us to keep any silver, gold, or jewelry, declaring in no uncertain terms that we must hand it over to the Red Army. I had two small diamond rings from my mother and one ring from Moshe that I hid from them anyway. But I decided to make use of the gold watch Moshe had left with me. I thought it would be most fitting to use it to buy weapons from the Soviets. Moshe would certainly have supported my decision. Many of our fighters were still unarmed, particularly the Jewish soldiers from the Red Army who had escaped German POW camps. Moshe's gold watch bought us seven rifles— a considerable addition to the arsenal of the independent Jewish partisan unit we hoped to become.

The Jewish partisans from the Voroshilov otriad were enthused by the general's decision to send us east and asked their commander to let them join the Jewish group. He agreed but was angry, punishing them by taking away all their weapons except two old rifles. Now we had ten or twelve more experienced veteran fighters, but they were unarmed.

Finally we were on our way: about 120 in all, almost half unarmed, mostly young men and women, but also some older people and even a few children. Siomka Rothenberg was our commander. Vaska the Russian navigated with a map and the help of more experienced partisans from the Voroshilov otriad. He also acted as our *politruk* (officer in charge of political education): every morning we stood at attention, as was apparently custom in the Red Army, and he would deliver a brief lecture on patriotism and ideology meant to boost our morale. He would always conclude with the same message: "We want to be an independent Jewish unit."

The journey east lasted for weeks. Our destination was somewhere south of Pinsk. Polesia is a vast area full of thickly grown forests and swampy marshlands lining both sides of the Prypeć River. The Prypeć flows east to west and empties into the Bug. There were few roads and the population was sparse. Some railroad tracks traversed east and west, but the area was largely impassable to motor vehicles.

It was late fall and the trees had shed their leaves. Winter was coming. It rained incessantly and the nights were colder. I was depressed, indifferent, and exhausted. We walked for hours at a time, for days on end, under gray skies, through bleak and endless forests, all bare and colorless. From time to time we would camp somewhere for a few days, but mostly we walked during the day and camped at night in the forest or in a village.

During the first days of our journey, we crossed the Brest-Kowel railroad track. The railroads were the lifeline of the Nazi Empire in the east, so they were naturally a prime target for the partisans and well-guarded by the Germans. To cross the tracks without being seen, we had to crawl.

Misha Omelinski, one of the veteran partisans who had joined us from the Voroshilov otriad, brought us to our crossing point and oversaw the operation. Two by two, we crawled across in the dark of night. By morning the whole group had made it safely across. Misha also managed to acquire weapons in villages we passed through, increasing our stock dramatically.

Time heals. Slowly my spirits mended. With time I got to know the newcomers from Voroshilov and became especially friendly with Misha. Even from the beginning I noticed he was gazing at me at every chance but too shy to make a move. I noticed he was very clean, well dressed, and neat. His gear was always well organized and his blanket always impeccably folded – I liked that too. Misha was eight years older than me, authoritative and experienced, with an air of self-confidence, yet gentle and caring. No wonder I fell in love with him.

We talked a lot and told one another what we had been through. He cared for me and asked endlessly how I was. I found out he was quite well known in our area because he had been part of the Jewish athletic club at Brest and a local soccer star. It seemed he was never cold, never wore a hat, and his shirtsleeves were always rolled up. Beyond all that, he was a veteran fighter and I felt safe and protected with him.

Little by little we were drawn to each other. When exactly did our romance begin? I think it was during our journey east at a camp site where we stayed for a few days. One lovely morning Misha showed up in a peasant's cart (by that time we had a few horses and carts acquired in the villages) and invited me on a romantic date, which was rather risky. I covered my head with a colorful kerchief borrowed from one of the girls so I would look like a peasant. We drove on dirt roads through fields, talked and laughed gaily, and then had a kind of picnic at the edge of a small grove.

Toward the end of October, we reached the area of the Dnieper-Bug canal, where three rivers join: the Bug, the Dnieper, and the Prypeć. There we made contact with the Molotov Brigade. To our great disappointment, we were told that we would not be an independent Jewish partisan unit but would be divided among three otriads of the brigade. Most of our group was attached to the Shishov otriad or the Kalinin otriad.[1]

A group of partisans, Molotov Brigade, Shishov otriad, Polesia 1943

Winter was coming and the *otriad*s were building their winter camps. We waited in an improvised camp until our winter quarters were ready. We began to adjust to our new situation as Jewish "soldiers" in a Soviet partisan unit. For women and girls without a father or brother, it was critical to find a fiancé or husband. We knew that Soviet partisans were a wild bunch and that without a male "patron" to protect us, we would be vulnerable. It was also important because they respected official family ties and would not separate couples who were engaged or married, or parents and their children. In no time, there were attachments, whether real or fictitious. Many of those attachments remained firm and even led to marriage after the war. I naturally chose Misha as my "patron." I now knew for certain there was someone who would look after and protect me.

The nights were already bitterly cold. To avoid sleeping on the frozen forest ground, we felled trees and made slightly raised wooden bedding, but still we were completely exposed to the wind and rain. Misha and I snuggled together under our coats and blankets. Finally, at the end of October or beginning of November 1943, our camp was ready. Thus began a new episode in our lives.

* * *

The Shishov otriad camp was in a thickly wooded area. The unit numbered about one hundred and fifty men structured militarily: three combat platoons comprising three squads of twelve men each, and an extra "logistics" platoon for those providing additional services. The living quarters were underground dugouts, called *zemlyanki* in Russian, covered by slanted roofs that jutted out slightly above ground but were camouflaged with branches and leaves to avoid detection from the air. Each squad slept in its own *zemlyanka*, and there were separate zemlyanki for the kitchen, command headquarters, officers, and various craftsmen.

A zemlyanka in the forests of Parczew

A typical squad zemlyanka was deep enough for an average man to stand in. It was about three meters wide and ten to fifteen meters long. The walls and floor were covered with wooden planks. One entered down a ladder at the narrow side of the rectangle. Along one of the walls stretched bed boards covered with straw bedding. Along the opposite wall were several wooden benches, a table, and a wood-burning stove whose chimney emitted its smoke through the roof. For light there was a "candle", a dish of lard in which a wick was lit. The heat from the stove was pleasant and was also used to boil drinking water. The dugout was small, crowded and not ventilated, but it did provide excellent shelter from the elements.

One zemlyanka I especially remember was that of Shlomo Boiman the tailor and Rubakha the cobbler. Both were

Jews; they provided the uniforms and boots for the camp. When we arrived at the camp, Rubakha made each of the women boots out of strips of leather, and Boiman sewed us trousers out of blankets. There was also a workshop to produce *volyanki*—one-size boots made of thick, waterproof felt—a bread bakery with an attached kitchen and mess hall, a pigpen, and a stable for horses. The partisans had dug a well that supplied water in abundance.

The logistics battalion was the largest and included a squad for the upkeep of horses and wagons. All noncombatants—most of the women and the older and younger people—were assigned jobs in the general upkeep of the camp.

Most of the partisans—the fighters and craftsmen—were Belorussians, generally young and from towns and villages in the area. Most reached the partisans after having been subjected to oppression at the hands of the Germans, and a few even brought family members with them: parents, wives, and younger siblings. All became part of the workforce. From time to time, former prisoners were recruited who had been on the German side and performed guard duty but deserted and returned to the Soviet side the first chance they got. The officers were Soviet military men, mostly Russians, who had been taken prisoner by the Germans but had escaped or become separated from their units and survived in the forests. Most were more educated and civilized than the other partisans.

The regular partisans were vulgar boors from the villages. I sometimes overheard them talking to each other and was amazed by their obscene language, shocked by their crude descriptions of sexual exploits, and their tall tales and superstitions. They would get drunk whenever they could get their hands on *samogon* (home-brewed vodka) from the villages.

Antisemitism was widespread among most of the Belorussians and many Russians. It was natural to them, an accepted truth, one they imbibed with their mothers' milk. Within the framework of the platoon, this antisemitism was not usually dangerous, but discrimination or antisemitic remarks or a degrading attitude were an everyday occurrence. We were a Jewish group, yet also foreign because we were Polish.[2] We were quite unified, and as we felt different from the Soviet partisans, we stuck together. Many an evening we would gather in Boiman and Rubakha's zemlyanka and talk in Yiddish or Polish, laugh, and sing popular Polish songs. This would outrage some of the other partisans. One evening somebody threw a grenade into the zemlyanka where we were gathered. It was a miracle we were not killed; the grenade didn't explode.

One day, the partisans brought a German prisoner to the camp, a slightly older man. He was scared and had been beaten. The Russians suggested giving him to the Jews (*Zhids*) as a prize. We could take revenge on those who had murdered our families, but on condition that he be killed by bayonet, not shot. None volunteered to do so, causing a barrage of insulting and demeaning comments, ridicule, and scorn.

Discipline in the camp was strict and cruel. Neglecting guard duty was punishable by death. One Jew who was caught asleep during guard duty was swiftly, convicted, and executed. I don't believe the punishment would have been as severe if he had not been Jewish. Now for the first time I was seeing up close what was called "The Soviet Paradise," and I became totally disillusioned.

When I witnessed the discrimination, the gross antisemitism, and the enormous gap between the status and conditions for officers and regular soldiers, I lost any lingering doubt I might have had about the Soviet regime and Communism. The reality I witnessed, and which was evident to anyone who looked, was proof of the glaring hypocrisy of the Soviet line. No one was fooled by the propaganda, patriotic lectures, heroic stories, and Stalin's speeches that we were subjected to every morning during roll call.

Immediately after roll call, we would go to our assigned tasks. Each platoon (*vzvod* in Russian) in turn would leave for three weeks of activity outside the camp; the two remaining platoons would guard the camp or perform short assignments and return to camp.

Most of the women were assigned to duties in logistics, but three joined combat squads: Andje Edelsberg, Rivka Weisbrod from Tomaszowka, and me. Our main job was to guard the camp. There were three guard posts outside the camp and one inside. The external ones were about one kilometer from the camp. The guards received their weapon from the duty officer and passed them on to the next guard. I would stand inside a trench in any weather, armed with a rifle, and do my best to stay awake.

We mainly needed to guard against Vlasov's men (POWs who joined the Germans) because the Germans rarely wandered the forests at night. The shift lasted four hours and I was petrified of falling asleep, so I would prepare a list of "thoughts" in advance that would help pass the time: One night, I recounted all the movies I had ever seen (not many); another night I recalled all the songs I knew.

Guard duty went on in all weather, of course. In winter, in the freezing cold, I would trundle through the snow to the guard post, wrapped in a coat, and wearing thick volyanki boots that reached mid-thigh. I would stomp my feet and rub my hands to avoid freezing. If the guard encountered a potential threat, the procedure was simple and universal. We would say: "Halt! Password!" then one warning shot, and if all that failed, effective fire. One stormy winter night I was standing guard and staring at the snow as it swirled around me. Visibility was poor—I could see only a few dozen meters ahead, and it was freezing. Suddenly I noticed a large black lump heading toward me in the night. I shouted, "*Stoy!*" ("Halt!"), but the only answer was the howling of the wind. The dark lump was heading toward me quickly and I thought it was a horse—I didn't see a rider, but someone had to be on it. I was alarmed but kept a cool head and acted according to orders: I cocked the rifle and shot one warning shot into the air. The shot sounded like cannon fire in the silent snowy forest. But the horse kept coming. Now I had no choice. I lifted the rifle to my shoulder and pulled the trigger. The butt struck my shoulder hard. I opened my eyes and the horse was gone. There was nothing there except the sweeping snow and howling wind. After some time, the duty officer came running.

"What happened?" he asked.

I told him there had been a horse galloping toward the guard post and my warnings weren't heeded. The next day the horse's body was found nearby. Then a few days later during morning roll call, I heard my name. The story of my run-in with the horse was part of the commander's morning pep talk on bravery. Overnight, I had become a Soviet heroine.

That was my one single act of military bravery during the whole war. I routinely stood guard for one shift every night (once or twice for a double shift when my replacement didn't show), and sometimes performed a day shift. I suffered from chronic fatigue and lack of sleep. When I wasn't on guard duty, I was required to help with all sorts of household tasks. Before breakfast and lunch, I would help in the kitchen. The women would sit together and peel mounds of potatoes. Sometimes I had to launder our squad soldiers' clothes and underwear. That was the hardest job, and I detested it most of all. I would boil a large pot of water and throw their filthy clothes in. Then I would fish them out one by one with a long pole and hang them out to dry on the tree branches.

* * *

Meals were served at least twice a day. We ate either in the mess-hall zemlyanka or, when the weather allowed, outdoors on long tables near the kitchen. Each squad would send someone to the kitchen, and he or she would return with a large, piping-hot bowl and set it on the table, with a few loaves of bread baked at the camp. The dish was invariably a thin cabbage soup with pieces of pork or lamb. Each of us would immediately pull a spoon out of his or her boot and try to scoop out a piece of meat. I had a combination spoon and fork, so I felt rich! After all the meat had been eaten, there was still some thin murky liquid and a bit of cabbage in the bowl. That "soup" would be fed to the pigs. One morning—I remember it was Yom

Kippur and we had intended to fast—Misha woke me up and said, "Come on, hurry up, they're serving green pea soup today." We ran to the kitchen and it was true—the watery cabbage soup had been replaced by a watery pea soup. We ate that new soup with gusto. The next day we got pea soup again, and the next, and the next—for three months.

Fresh fruits and vegetables were something we never had. Once or twice Misha brought me a "box of candies": a honeycomb that he robbed from wild bees. He had become an expert at getting honeycombs when he had been wandering alone through the forests before he found the partisans. I would spoon some of the honey out of the honeycomb and drink it with *kipitok* (boiled water), a treat for angels.

However, our food was usually so lacking in vitamins that in addition to my sores that never healed I came down with scurvy. My gums and tongue were so swollen and sore that I couldn't eat and could hardly speak. I was sent to the doctor. The doctor (who was actually a vet) occupied a rather lavish zemlyanka that he shared with a photographer, Fanny.[3] The zemlyanka had windows, curtains, and even a carpet. He examined me rather halfheartedly and said that from then on, I would get officers' food. I discovered that the officers got excellent food: real soups, meatballs, fried potatoes. But the "cure" was a joke. My mouth was so swollen that I was unable to eat the officers' first-rate food.

When it came to bathing, it was a rare event for the partisans. However, the women did manage to bathe from time to time. We would go as a group to one of the zemlyanki, which we would take over for the occasion.

One woman would stand guard while the others would heat water on a campfire and we would wash ourselves.

* * *

One cold winter night, while I was guarding inside the camp, the duty officer Sashka felt sorry for me and invited me to warm up in his zemlyanka. Sashka "Cossack" was a Soviet soldier who had agreed to collaborate with the Germans while in a POW camp. He had been assigned to guard the railway tracks, and at the first opportunity defected and joined the ranks of the partisans.

We were warming up in his zemlyanka , drinking kipitok and chatting. When we ran out of topics of conversation, Sashka said, "Let me tell you a nice tale." It was actually a terribly sad tale about a poor young man living in a capitalistic country. He was so hungry that he stole a loaf of bread from a bakery and was sentenced to twenty years in prison. The story started to sound more and more familiar, and suddenly it struck me what Sashka Cossack was doing.

"Wait a minute, Sashka," I interrupted, "but that isn't just any story. That is a well-known book called *Les Miserables* by the famous French author Victor Hugo."

Sashka looked at me dumbfounded. "Do you know that tale?" he asked.

"Of course," I answered, "I read it in school."

Sashka was amazed to no end. And from then on his esteem for me grew. He considered me part of the *Intellegentzia* and treated me fairly the whole time I was in the partisans.

There is more to the story of Sashka Cossack; it is connected to that of Yula Tsipperstein. Yula was one of several Jewish women in our otriad (in addition to our Polish group) from around Pinsk. She lived with a platoon commander, Kokshin.

Yula was about my age, a pretty redhead from the town of Pohost in Polesia. During our time together, we became friends and naturally shared our experiences. Every Jew who survived and made it to the partisans had an awful story to tell, but Yula's was more shocking than most. On the day the Jews of her village were massacred, she was standing naked in front of the pit, along with hundreds of other Jews, and the murderers' rifles were aimed at her. Shots were fired and she fell into the pit, on top of the corpses of those shot before her. More shots were fired, and more corpses fell on top of her and covered her. This went on for some time. She was in the pit, but not dead. The bullet meant for her had grazed her forehead. The shooting continued all day long until the killing for the day was done. Yula squirmed her way out, pushing the corpses aside with all her strength until she managed to climb out.

Naked, wounded, and half crazed with terror, Yula wandered through the forest until she came to a village. She knocked at the door of the first house she came to and asked for water and clothing. The villagers fed her, clothed her, and showed her the way that might lead her to the partisans, so she went. That was how a partisan reconnaissance group commanded by Kokshin found her. He was a lieutenant from Leningrad and took Yula under his wing and protected her.

After the liberation, they married in Pinsk, where he got a good job in the local government. The two were able to have a fairly comfortable life. As part of his duties, Kokshin was in charge of collecting the crop quotas from the surrounding villages. One day, accompanied by another clerk, he went to one of the villages, entered one of the houses, put his revolver on the table, and sat down to talk to the peasant. Suddenly three armed men burst in. One of them was Sashka Cossack.

It turned out that Sashka, like all who had collaborated with the enemy, had been assigned as punishment to a battalion that was sent to the front. But Sashka escaped and returned to the forests. His treatment had turned him into an anti-Soviet partisan.

"Sashka," said Kokshin. "What? Are you going to kill me?"

"I will kill you like a dog," said Sashka, and he did.

Yula was left alone in Pinsk, in her ninth month of pregnancy. Sometime later, she married a Jewish man and they went to America.[4]

* * *

The year 1943 ended under a heavy blanket of snow, and 1944 began. The New Year, one of the few holidays in the Soviet calendar, was felt in our camp. All who hadn't left on assignment got the day off and immediately started in on their favorite pastime: drinking samogon. They ran all around the camp, drinking and singing at full volume. In the evening, near my zemlyanka, I suddenly ran into a rowdy bunch in high spirits. The revelers greeted me and wished me a happy New Year.

"Happy New Year to you, too," I responded politely but cautiously.

"Sonya (that's what most of them called me), come toast the New Year with us!" one of them said.

"But I don't drink," I said. "I can't drink."

"You have to! Today is a holiday. Drink with us," the fellow said, and all the others surrounded me with cries of encouragement.

I felt I had no choice. One of the partisans handed me a tin cup and poured a hefty shot of samogon. I took one sip and started to choke. I swallowed the burning liquid and felt like my insides were on fire. My hands were shaking as I gave him back the cup, and with that the partisans burst out laughing. It seemed they enjoyed the spectacle.

"More! Drink some more!" the fellow shouted, and the other partisans followed in chorus, "More! Drink! Drink!"

I hesitated and felt confused and intimidated. The chorus around me was getting louder and louder. "Drink! Drink! Drink!" I raised the cup and drank. Vodka was dripping down my chin, my mouth was burning, and the world was spinning. I finally tossed the cup aside and ran out to my zemlyanka. Their raucous laughter rang in my ears until I reached the entrance.

That night I slept it off like a drunkard. It was the first time in my life—and the last—I ever drank vodka.

* * *

Throughout the whole time we never forgot that war was raging about us. During morning roll call we listened to the news from Radio Moscow and heard about our colossal victories, about the *katyusha*—the doomsday weapon that was the scourge of the enemy—and about the advance of the front westward toward us.

Misha took part in operations outside the camp for weeks at a time. When he came back for a week or two of rest, he would recount what happened. I am not sure he told me everything, but enough of what I heard scared me to death. What would happen if I lost him?

Misha's commanders admired him greatly and the other partisans respected him because of his fighting ability. He had no problem drinking with them and he would amuse them with card tricks. He got along with them naturally and was accepted as one of them despite his minimal Russian and his Jewish-Polish origins. Perhaps the respect he gained from them had an influence on their behavior toward me.

During those weeks that the partisans spent outside the camp, they would pass through the villages under their control, gather information and intelligence, punish collaborators, make sure the crop quotas (the "contingent") were delivered to the partisans on time, and occasionally raid an isolated German post, attack Germans at village railroad stations, or ambush German guards. The partisans' crowning glory was sabotaging railroad tracks, which were the lifeline of the Nazi empire in the east.

Misha was an experienced and trained sapper and would lay explosives under rail tracks. One night, a squad set out to blow up a train and Misha went with them as the sapper. Apparently, the mission failed and the train was not derailed because the bomb failed to explode. In any case, a few of the partisans involved returned to the camp late that night—and Misha was not with them!

"Our Mishka has fallen," said one of the men.

I ran out to my zemlyanka, shut the door and threw myself on the bed board. I didn't cry, but I will never forget the feeling of shock and horror and the terrible thoughts that were starting to gnaw at me, that I was cursed, and anyone who loved me was certain to die. But those thoughts didn't last long. Soon someone knocked on the door and yelled out, "They're back! They're back!" I didn't move an inch. What did I care that they were back if Misha wasn't with them? And then minutes later the door opened and there was Misha, standing there, soiled, smiling—and safe and sound.

Little by little we were learning to dare to hope. Was the end really near? Sometime mid-winter we were taught to hear the front approaching: if you laid you ear on the frozen ground, you could feel a kind of dull, distant tremor. The front was indeed getting closer.

One cold night at the end of winter, the whole otriad went out on a mission. Everyone was ordered to take part, including the women and the logistics people. Each of us received a small demolition slab about the size and shape of a bar of soap. Our mission was to blow up the tracks of the Brest-Pinsk railroad line. We walked through the forest for a long time until we reached our designated section of the track, and each of us placed his or her explosive close to the metal track, keeping twenty or thirty meters between explosives. From that night, on the track was out of order for quite some time.

Sometime around March, we started to hear the thunder of the front. It sounded dull and distant, like an approaching storm. A rumor spread that several otriads had already started to fold up camp and head east. Partisan activities were becoming more frequent and intense and the battles with the Germans fiercer. Many partisans were killed or injured in those battles, but casualties among Jews were few. The injured were evacuated deep into Russia from an airstrip that the partisans had set up near the village of Khydra. Reinforcements, medical supplies, and weapons from the Red Army also reached us via the airstrip.

One morning, someone came running and called me to go with him to the otriad headquarters. Near that zemlyanka stood a cart driven by a partisan from another unit, and beside him sat a woman and a child I had never seen before. The woman was looking for Misha Omelinski.

"I was told he is at this otriad," she said.

I told her Misha was on a mission, but that I was his girlfriend.

"I'm from Kobryń," the woman said. "I knew Misha's brother, Nathan, and I want you to know that my daughter and I are both alive thanks to him."

I knew that Misha's family had been expelled from Brest to nearby Kobryń. Nathan was the third of five siblings, and Misha always said he was the most accomplished of all of them. It turned out that Nathan was an important figure in the partisans in that area near Kobryń.

But the woman had come to deliver devastating news: Nathan had been killed in a skirmish with the Germans.

We only learned the whole story many years later in Israel when, after extensive efforts, Misha managed to meet with the sole survivor from the incident in which his brother had been killed. Nathan and his men were operating in one of the villages and spent the night in a house at the edge of the village. One of the villagers must have informed on them as the Germans surrounded the house and opened fire. All the partisans in the house were killed except the one who was on guard. He managed to escape when the attack began. He was the one who told Misha the story.

* * *

At the beginning of April there was still no sign that winter was ending. The weather was cold and stormy for days. The zemlyanki started to fill with water, and every day we needed to raise our bed boards a little higher. Day and night, we could hear the ever-increasing cannon thunder from the front booming louder and louder.

At that point, large German forces raided our forest. We found out that the Germans had sent elite units[5] to clear the forests of partisans in preparation for their confrontation with the Red Army.

The otriad was evacuated in haste. All combatants set out on their missions and the logistics people were sent to another location. A fierce battle took place not far from our camp and we incurred some fifty casualties. My friend Andje, who had previously decided to be a combat soldier, was injured and evacuated to Russia.

Only a few remained in camp: one officer, two or three fighters, Rivka Bialla[6] from Tomaszowka, and me. I don't remember why Rivka and I had remained; I think we had volunteered to stay and bake bread for the whole otriad.

We were there alone for a day or two, baking bread, guarding and listening to the raging battle. On the third day a partisan reconnaissance squad led by Officer Kolya came into the camp. There were five fighters in the group, including Avigdor Shporrer and Misha. They were to accompany all of us to the otriad's new location and make sure no one was left behind. Misha had noticed German tracks near our camp, so the reconnaissance commander decided to evacuate us with not a moment to lose.

Our commander heard the news, said not a word, and with a poker face went toward his horse, spread a small saddle rug on its back, mounted silently, galloped off, and disappeared. Rivka and I took a loaf of bread each and walked off with the reconnaissance squad.

We walked briskly through the forest. We had not gone far from the camp when we suddenly froze in our tracks. Only a few dozen meters ahead, we saw a stream through the trees and a small bridge crossing it. Three men were standing by the side of the stream with their backs to us. At first we only saw the white camouflage color of their uniforms, but one minute later we noticed their caps. "Germans!" someone whispered, and at that moment we all ran in the opposite direction. We ran as fast as we could. I remember Misha running behind me and telling me to run zigzag. Soon there were only the four of us— Rivka, Avigdor, Misha, and I—and finally we emerged from the thicket of trees and came into a large and exposed clearing.

A wide winding path led to another forest a few kilometers away. It was a swampy marshland, and the path was a black stretch of muddy bog. Along the path was a long procession of peasants who had abandoned their villages in fear of the approaching Germans. Carts were sinking in the mud and people were laboring to pull them out. It was a scene of total chaos. Men, women, and children—with their carts, cows, and squealing pigs— were all screaming at each other and trying furiously to move along the path.

We, too, moved along slowly and painfully. A thin layer of ice covered the watery path in many places, and if you trod on the ice and it broke, your foot would sink into the icy water up to your knee. Our boots were waterlogged, which made it even harder. In some places the path crossed rushing water and you had to balance yourself and walk across planks of wood. As balance had never been my strength, Misha and Avigdor found two long branches that served as walking sticks and I was able to cross over. At one point, Misha noticed that I was still carrying the loaf of bread.

"Are you nuts?" he said. "Get rid of it already." But I couldn't just throw away a loaf of bread, so I placed it on one of the peasants' carts.

We plodded on like that in the mud and ice the whole day, and toward evening we ran into members of our reconnaissance squad. Rivka and I were sent to a nearby village where our otriad's logistics company was stationed, and Misha and Avigdor were sent to join the rest of the otriad.

We were relieved and happy to join our logistics people in the village. My feet hurt and I was frozen and exhausted. I took off my boots, poured the water out, and was looking forward to a nice long rest when suddenly the cry was heard: "We're heading out." Soon I found myself plodding along in the mud, this time in a procession of partisans and loaded carts, all moving steadily south. Evening came and we were suddenly shrouded in heavy darkness. I staggered forward like a blind woman, the wind raging, in a heavy snowstorm.

I have no idea how long we walked that way. At a certain point I asked a carter to let me sit on his cart, but he said it was impossible—his horses were exhausted. The carter advised that I grab onto the cart, which I did and was somehow dragged along forward. Hours passed. The snow pelted my face. I thought I would be walking on like that forever. I could feel my strength ebbing. I walked on, eyes closed, deathly tired, and was probably walking in my sleep.

All of a sudden the cart stopped, and I came fully awake at once, my eyes wide open. The procession had come to a standstill. The snow had stopped; I even imagined it was not as dark. A moment of silence. Then shouts from far ahead of us, "Hurray! Hurray!" I could almost distinguish shadows or outlines of people and carts ahead of me with white snow in the background. The shouting not only continued but came rolling toward us, and then all those around me were shouting, too, "Hurray! Hurray!"

Suddenly, out of the darkness came a long black mass, swaying, moving forward, bayonets pointed toward the dark heaven. It was a Red Army unit.

---

1. The Molotov Brigade consisted of four otriads: Shishov, Kalinin, Lazov, and Kotozov. The Kalinin camp was not far away, and the Jews from there would visit us.

2. The western portion of Belorussia (including the region of Pinsk) belonged to Poland until the war.

3. Fanny Lazebnik, a young Jewish woman from the town of Lenin in Belorussia, was the brigade photographer. After the war she lived in Canada.

4. I heard the end of the story from Yula herself after the liberation, when we were living in Pinsk. My relationship with Yula continued until recently, and we even saw each other in Israel when she came to visit relatives.

5. Waffen-SS, the military branch of the SS.

6. After the liberation, Rivka married Avigdor Shporrer and lived in Israel.

8

HOMEWARD

April 1944-August 1945

We soon left the forest. Soviet soldiers could be seen everywhere—standing, marching, singing, working. Soldiers were directing the crowds along the muddy paths. We were sent toward a large village not far away. We crossed a bridge and entered it, and then were directed to an abandoned house. Once inside, we collapsed on the floor in total exhaustion and slept like logs.

Liberation! This was the moment we had not dared to dream of for the past four and a half years.

We reached that moment drained of strength, barely daring to hope, barely alive, the sole remnants of families and whole towns. The Soviets were beside themselves with joy—they had homes to return to—at least most did. We felt relieved, a kind of limpness. The nightmare was finally over, but it was not joy we felt.

The name of the village where we were staying was Kuchecka Wola in the province of Volyn in the Ukraine. It was April 1944.

When we awoke the next morning, the weather was clear and cold. We settled into an abandoned house. There was a typical traditional village type cooker in the kitchen called a *petchka* with a deep oven. You used a long wooden pole to place pots or clay dishes inside. We got washed as best we could, made some breakfast, and looked outside.

The Soviet army was moving west through the village, either by foot or on wheels and tracks. For hours on end, the traffic moved along toward the front line. We stood in the street, looked at the soldiers' faces, and out of boredom tried to guess which faces were Jewish. We would test ourselves by going up to the individual in question and whisper a word in Yiddish that all Jews knew: "*Amcha*?"[1] If the soldier was Jewish, he would answer "Amcha."

A few days later, the rest of our otriad arrived at the village. Red Army officers stationed in the area soon learned that there was a partisan group in the village that included Jews. One day, a general invited us to dinner. A group of us women walked to the neighboring village and arrived at his headquarters. A white tablecloth and pretty dishes had been set by the general's aide, and we all sat at the long table with several officers. It was a meal fit for kings, such as we had not eaten for years. After dinner, we told the officers about ourselves, the mass extermination of our people, and Sobibor. They then offered to put us up for the night and prepared straw bedding in one of the rooms in the house. During the night, a few of the soldiers came in and tried to get into bed with us, but we screamed and managed to push them out. To prevent a recurrence, and also to keep warm, we cuddled together in our coats and fell asleep. In the morning they treated us to a hearty breakfast, after which we walked back to our village with light hearts and full bellies.

During our stay, we were summoned to an office and each was given a "Partisan Certificate." We entered the office one at a time, the officer at his desk gave us the certificate, and we signed and left. I was about to sign when I naïvely asked if I could sign in Polish. The officer was startled and shouted, "No Polish. This is not Poland. Sign in Russian or don't sign at all!" I asked if I could come back a little later so I could practice my signature in Russian, then returned thirty minutes later. I signed and received my certificate.

That document was worth gold. Wherever we presented it to a policeman, officer, soldier, or NKVD[2] official, we were treated with respect and helped with whatever we asked.

The document certified that Sara, daughter of David Lustigman, was a partisan in the Shishov Otriad of the Molotov Brigade from May 1943 to April 1944. All persons were requested to aid the bearer of the certificate with any necessary arrangements, work or otherwise. It was signed April 25, 1944 in Kuchecka Wola, on behalf of the Belorussia Headquarters of the Soviet Partisan Movement.

After that they started to send us off to various places. Most of the fit partisans were recruited into the Red Army and stationed at Vinnitsa in the Ukraine. Misha and a few of the veteran partisans were sent east to the Belorussia Headquarters of the Partisan Movement to return all the property of the otriad: carts, animals, arms, tools, and all other equipment.

We women were told they were sending us to Donbass in the Ukraine, a town renowned for its coal mines. We were so upset that we decided to organize and demand to be sent elsewhere. We went to the officer in charge of assignments and stated our case. We said we were all Polish, had been fighters in the partisans, had all lost all our family, and demanded to stay in this area until Poland was liberated and we could go home. The officer listened to us in silence and, to our surprise, he agreed. Our assignment was canceled. We then asked to go to the nearby town of Maniewicze because a colleague of ours who had been wounded in battle was there and we wanted to take care of her. He agreed to that, too, and promised to arrange travel permits for us.

There was another reason we wanted to go to Maniewicze, besides that our friend Andje was in a military hospital there recovering from her injuries. We knew that a woman from Włodawa, Leah (Lisa) Saperstein, was living there. Leah was tall, strong, and assertive. Her husband had previously emigrated to South America, and in the war she had been in the Kalinin otriad. In the forests her young son had become ill and died and she was left alone with her eight-year-old daughter Lusha. After the liberation she found work in Maniewicze in the train station shop. We knew she would be able to help us get settled.

A few days later, we received the necessary travel permits and got ready to go. The provisions for our journey were a bag of semolina (a type of flour made from wheat) and a small cloth wrapper containing a modest amount of sugar. Sugar! We hadn't tasted that delicacy for years. I sprinkled a little of the sugar on a slice of bread and ate it ravenously, like cake.

We set out on foot early in the morning. There were five of us women, all from the Shishov otriad; Rivka Bialla, the two Weisbrod sisters from Tomaszowka, Peska Kutcher from Włodawa, and me. We traveled the whole day on village paths and by evening reached the town of Rafaluwka, where we lodged with an ex-partisan. We boiled our semolina in water, sprinkled sugar on top, set our bowls on the table near the window, took our spoons out of our boots, and, feeling happy, sat down to eat.

We were still eating when we heard a loud blast. The lights went out and the window near us shattered, with the splintered glass bloodying Peska's face. In alarm we ran outside. Townspeople were running about and clouds of smoke filled the air. A big fire had broken out somewhere nearby. We ran out of the town and found shelter in the forest along with hundreds of others, and there we spent the night. The following morning, we returned to the house and discovered that a Soviet plane had been shot down by mistake above Rafaluwka and crashed in the center of the town and burst into flames, destroying a few houses. When we passed by the crash site in the morning, we saw the remains of the plane and the charred bodies of the pilots as well as the surrounding burned-out houses.

We left Rafaluwka and continued to Maniewicze. Leah already knew we were coming and prepared a place for us to stay with her: an abandoned house near a factory that produced floorboards. Nobody had wanted to live there because it was so close to the factory, but for us, it was good enough. Somehow, we improvised furnishings: we laid a large cupboard with its back facing up and used it as a bed. We dragged benches and utensils from other abandoned dwellings and settled in.

Leah and her daughter, Lusha, joined us, and shortly afterward, Andje did too. She had recovered quickly and was released from hospital. To support ourselves, we laundered uniforms for soldiers stationed in the town or passing through. They paid us in salt, which we learned could be used as currency and traded for other commodities. With salt, we bought bread, meat, and other supplies. Meanwhile, Andje started to work with Leah at the train-station shop.

It didn't take long for us to find out another reason our house had been abandoned. The front line was not far away—the battle for the city of Kovel, the province capital, was still raging. The city was bombed nearly every night, and people were afraid to live next to a factory that might be a target. We were too frightened to sleep inside the house at night, so we slept in nearby trenches or elsewhere.

Life was hard. We slaved away laundering and cooking, carried buckets of water, and every evening we left to look for a safe place to sleep. Meanwhile Leah had found a lover, a Jewish officer named Melamed, and the two would stay in the house at night while we went to look for shelter. Apparently, they were not afraid. When Leah was with Melamed, I looked after Lusha.

As time passed, we got a reputation in the town as Jewish partisans. Many visited us and brought gifts, especially

Jewish officers. The mayor would sometimes invite us to sleep in the shelter in his house. One time, when we were on our way to the mayor's house, we were caught in a bombing attack. Flares lit up the sky and the night skies were bright as day. German dive bombers swooped down with a terrible shrill whistle, dropped their bombs, and sprayed the streets with machine-gun fire. It was a miracle we escaped unharmed and made it to the mayor's shelter.

Another time, we were invited to sleep at the home of a Polish woman we knew from town. Her house was on the outskirts of town, and a few of us set out in the late afternoon with Lusha. It was a gorgeous summer day and we were looking forward to a pleasant evening, a hearty meal, and a tranquil night. We walked along barefoot, in light summer dresses, youthful and good looking. A long military train, full and overflowing with soldiers, stood at the train station, and I clearly remember their stares and whistles.

We arrived at our destination safely, enjoyed a delicious dinner of hot soup, and went to bed in the hayloft. We undressed and stretched out on the warm fragrant hay as if on cloud nine and quickly fell asleep.

However, our restful sleep was short lived. In the middle of the night we were woken by a tremendous boom. We opened our eyes and instead of rafters above us, saw a sky full of stars. I was so alarmed that I ran out like a blind woman. Running barefoot in the harvested fields, my feet were sore from the stubble. Soon I calmed down and caught my breath. Suddenly I remembered: Lusha! I ran back to the house and looked for her everywhere. We all circled the house and called her name. After some time we found her, safe and sound. We later learned that a stray bomb had exploded a few meters from the house, creating a deep crater in the ground and blowing off the roof.

We also met Jews living in and around town, and they helped us as much as they could. Yankele Lederman and Bollek Huberman (whose brother Yekhezkel had been drafted into the Red Army) were stationed as policemen in the towns and villages in the area. When they found out we were there, they would sometimes visit.

One day, Yankele came over, and in the evening when we left to look for shelter from the bombing, he remained in the house. That night the bombing was particularly heavy. Near the station, a train laden with ammunition caught fire, and the munitions kept exploding and burning for hours. We returned to the house in the morning and found Yankele sleeping like a baby—and next to his bed was a whole sack of salt. What a treasure! There was enough salt to provide for us for some weeks. Apparently during the bombing Yankele had gone to the train station, taking advantage of the general chaos, stolen into one of the warehouses, and taken a sack of salt.

Summer was nearly over, and autumn was in the air. Our group started to disperse. Our boyfriends had found jobs and settled down in various places, so they came for their girlfriends. Avigdor Shporrer came from Pinsk and took Rivka there with him. Rubakha came for Peska. Misha and I had been writing to each other, so I knew that after having returned all the otriad's equipment, he had declared he was a professional driver. He was sent to work for the Central Committee of the Communist Party of Belorussia in Gomel until the eventual liberation of the republic capital, Minsk. In his letters, Misha wrote that he was pleased with the work and that he was living in a dormitory for party workers, eating in their dining room, and lacking nothing. They even gave him clothing from America.

Then one day, with no warning, he showed up. Through the window I saw a man coming toward the house, someone I didn't know. His gait was familiar, but his clothes were odd. He was wearing a lightweight jacket sticking out over dark blue trousers with lots of pockets. "Oh my God, it's Misha!" I exclaimed and ran out the door.

He had received permission to travel to bring his "wife" to Gomel and acquired all the necessary documents. He even had the foresight to bring five hundred rubles he had saved to cover all necessary expenses.

Evening came, and we set out to look for a nice place in the forest to sleep. We had to search for a long time because the forest was full of Soviet forces: soldiers, vehicles, trenches, bunkers, and barbed wire. We finally found a quiet spot, lay down on the forest floor, and covered ourselves with our coats. After I fell asleep, Misha covered my head with his coat so the flares wouldn't wake me.

In the middle of the night, however, the earth rumbled below me and ear-shattering bombs exploded above. I awoke in a panic, in the dark, threw the coat off my head, and a blinding light suddenly glared in my eyes.

The forest was being bombed. I got up and started running like mad. Misha ran after me, shouting, and only after some time was he able to catch up and stop my crazed run. We finally managed to find a Soviet army bunker and hid there until morning.

That day, we went to the marriage registrar's office of Maniewicze, where we presented our documents, filled out a form and were married, with Rubakha and Peska signing as our witnesses. Shortly after, we left the building as husband and wife.[3]

The next morning, we took the train to Sarny, a stop on the Kiev-Kowel line. From there, we planned to get the train to Gomel. We had a few hours to wait for our train, so we took a walk around town. A stream flowed through the town center and we walked alongside until we came to a peaceful green spot. We sat and dangled our feet in the water and opened our cans of food, which we ate with slices of bread. It was a nice interlude.

It was soon time to go back to the station and buy our tickets to Gomel. Misha presented his travel permit and, when asked to show identification, presented his partisan certificate. The clerk studied the documents carefully and, after a while, said, "On one document your name is Moisei (Moshe) Omelinski and on the other it is Michail."

In the general witch hunt atmosphere that pervaded the Soviet Union in recently liberated areas close to the front, every discrepancy in a document was enough to warrant suspicion of espionage. Banners were posted all over warning the population against possible enemy spies. We explained that we were Poles, ex-partisans, just married, and on our way to the party center in Gomel. We said there must have been a mistake in one of the documents.

To no avail. Our explanations fell on deaf ears. The ticket clerk called an armed soldier standing guard at the station. We were led to a small room and the door was locked.

What now? Even the slightest suspicion of espionage was enough to sentence a person to a long imprisonment in Siberia or the gulag. Worse still, in time of war, even the local junior officer was authorized to execute the most insignificant "spy" without a trial.

All sorts of frightful scenarios went through our minds. Eventually Misha got up and called to the sentry. They spoke in whispers and Misha gave him all the money we had left of the five hundred rubles. The guard opened our door, looked around, and let us go. The train had not left the station, so we ran aboard, but without tickets and travel permits, we were vulnerable.

It was a nightmare of a journey. The distance between Maniewicze and Gomel was about five hundred kilometers, which would normally take almost a week by train. Every time a ticket inspector came by, we hid in the restrooms. Not only that, but I started to feel ill. I had a stomachache that gradually got worse, diarrhea that was more and more frequent, and nausea and dizziness. At the next station where we got off to change trains, I could barely walk. Now there was blood in my stool—a clear symptom of dysentery.

For the rest of the journey we tried to hop on cargo trains, but it wasn't easy. We would get on a train, such as one transporting logs, and then wait hours for it to leave, only to find it was going the wrong direction or leaving the next day. Or we would get on the right train but have to get off to run to the restroom. The trains in general were slow, infrequent, and made dozens of stops. And you couldn't depend on the schedules at all.

Food was another problem. We hardly ate anything the whole time, and at train stations along the way we could only get boiled drinking water (*kipytok*) since it was free. On one of the freight trains there was a group of soldiers traveling alongside us. When they saw we weren't eating or drinking—we were too proud to ask for handouts—one of the soldiers gave us some toast.

The track went east for some distance, and at a railway intersection about two hundred kilometers west of Kiev, we turned north and entered Belorussia. We got off at Kalinkovichi, about seventy kilometers east of Gomel, and headed to the station cafeteria. It was half empty and we sat down at a rough wooden table, trying to decide what to do. I was at the end of my rope, but finally with the little strength I had left, I called to the shop assistant and told her I was very sick, had no money, and could use a cup of tea. The salesgirl took one look at me and must have understood what bad shape I was in. She said not a word and brought me tea. Misha and I sat at the table in silence. I drank my tea, and he sipped his kipytok. At another nearby table was a man who kept staring at us as if wondering who we were. I had kept my eye on him but had no energy to even think about who he might be. Finally, he got up and came over to our table and asked in a low voice, "Amcha?"

"Amcha," we answered.

"Where are you from?" he asked.

"From Poland. We are on our way to Gomel."

The man sat down at our table, and as was the custom for Jews, we told each other about our lives. We told him briefly about ourselves and he told us he was from Bialystoka but his wife was from Kalinkovichi. He had only recently come back with her to her hometown. When he heard how sick I was, he wanted to help.

"My wife works at the first aid center at the train station," he said. "She will be able to help you."

He took us there, and his wife examined me and gave me an opium solution to ease the stomach pain. In the evening, we went with them to their home. They lived at the outskirts of town in a house belonging to another family and had a narrow alcove with only a curtain for privacy. The wife helped me bathe a bit and made us soup and a vinaigrette salad. It was all wonderfully delicious, especially as we hadn't eaten properly for days. The next day the couple gave us bottles of water and some money and helped us board the right train. In a few hours we were in Gomel.

But we were in for a surprise. We learned that the Red Army had liberated Minsk, the capital of the republic. The party headquarters and all its departments were gone from Gomel and had relocated there. That meant we had to get to Minsk—more than three hundred kilometers by train.

Our immediate concern was to find a place to sleep. Fortunately, Misha remembered that he knew a Jewish family that had recently returned from Siberia—a father, mother, and grown daughter—and as Misha had done them some favors, they always treated him kindly. We decided to ask them to put us up for the night. They did so, but only begrudgingly. They let us sleep on the floor as if doing us a great favor. Misha was stunned. I surmised their attitude might be because they had hoped he would marry their daughter.

The next day, we were on our way to Minsk. We changed trains about halfway, in Bobruysk, but the little money we had from the couple in Kalinkovichi was gone. Not only that, but the train was packed. We had no choice: when the doors closed, we climbed up the steps leading to one of the cars outside the doors and held on to the handles. We traveled this way for hours. I have no idea how I managed considering how weak, hungry, and sick I still was. The train pulled into Minsk at 5 a.m.

After a brief rest at the station, we set out to find the party headquarters. The streets were almost empty except for an occasional worker on the way to work. Those we met pointed us in the direction of the main street and told us to take it to the end.

We found the main street, which went on for kilometers, and kept walking. On both sides of the street were scorched buildings, four or five stories high. The walls were destroyed and blackened with soot, with burned metal rods sticking out and windows that were black empty holes. The street itself was scattered with rubble. Before retreating, the Germans had bombed the whole length of the main street and only one building was miraculously spared—the Government House.

NKVD agents stood at each corner and checked documents. We showed them our partisan certificates and they nodded in approval, adding with a smile, "*Molodiets*! (Well done!)" before letting us pass.

The street seemed to go on forever. I finally sat down on the steps of a bombed-out building and said to Misha, "I cannot walk anymore. You go and find the place and come back for me." He did, and about a half hour later an American-made jeep pulled up with Misha and a colleague inside. I got inside and we went to the Communist Party Headquarters of Belorussia.

That was our honeymoon.

* * *

It was already winter when we arrived in Minsk. While we were waiting for our lodging to be arranged, Misha continued to sleep at the dormitory for party workers. I lived with a colleague of his named Ingberg, who was an ex-partisan from Drohicyzn. His wife was very hospitable and took such good care of me that I recovered from the dysentery quickly. The Ingbergs lived in one room in a poor neighborhood quite far from the city center in a dwelling that accommodated many people. The wife worked as a seamstress for party members and other influential people, and during the two weeks I stayed there I helped with her work. Again, I noticed the hypocrisy of the communist regime: garments that were sent to the Soviet Union from America found their way to party activists and their wives. Mrs. Ingberg made her living doing alterations for the top echelon.

After about two weeks we received our own room not far from the Ingbergs. It was a happy occasion, and when we got there and knocked on the door, it was opened by a mean looking one-eyed old woman with hardly any teeth —just like a wicked witch in a fairy tale. We told her we were supposed to have a room at her place. She looked us up and down and asked, "*Yevrei* [Hebrews]?"

When we didn't reply she raised her arms and declared, "I won't have Jews living with me."

We returned to the Ingbergs and Misha notified the party headquarters that the landlady refused to let us have the room. By the time the landlady was forced to relent, it had already been taken by an officer and his wife. The whole house was fully occupied and only the kitchen was available. Misha brought a bed from work and placed it in a corner of the kitchen. The kitchen contained a cooker, a table and chairs, a barrel for making sauerkraut, and utensils. There was no heater and the cold was unbearable. Nights when Misha slept there, we cuddled somehow under the fur coat he had from work, but nights when he worked, I simply froze.

The kitchen was the first room when you entered the house, so we got to see everything going on as the residents headed down the corridor from the kitchen to one of the four rooms. In the first room lived the old couple who owned the house and their retarded daughter. The old man would take his neighbors' cows to pasture, and in return they gave him milk that he would sell at market. In the second room, which was supposed to be ours, was the Soviet officer and his wife. On more than one occasion, the officer would come home drunk late at night and his wife would drag him through the kitchen. The third room was home to another of the owners' daughters, who had recently returned from the *kolkhoz* (collective farm) where she lived with two young children. The last room served as a home and workplace for the owners' third daughter, an attractive young girl who received "clients" from all walks of life. All the occupants and visitors passed through the kitchen on their way to their rooms.

At that time, every house in the Soviet Union had a special register, called "The House Book," in which all occupants had to list their names and places of employment. NKVD officials would make periodic visits to check the books and make sure no one was hiding spies or state enemies. When we moved in, the landlady handed me "The House Book" and told me to sign in as required by law. But I did not have a job, so I couldn't register. I immediately went to the Employment Bureau and presented my partisan certificate and asked for a job. The clerk replied there were many available jobs but that I couldn't be employed as I was a Polish citizen.

"So what happens next?" I asked. "How can I register in the House Book where I live?"

The officials had no answer. "Come back in two weeks," they said.

I went home empty handed, with no job and no way to register.

One day, two NKVD policemen came for a routine inspection. When they were done, saw my partisan certificate, said their customary "Molodiets," and were about to leave, the landlady came running.

"Wait," she said, "this one isn't registered."

"Why aren't you registered?" one of them asked severely.

"I don't have a job," I said.

"What? What do you mean you don't have a job? You need to go to the employment bureau and get work," he said sternly.

"I have already been there. They said it was impossible because I am a Polish citizen, and they told me to come back in two weeks."

The same thing happened over and over, every time they came to inspect—the same questions and the same dead end.

The greatest difficulty, however, was hunger. We depended on Misha's income for food, but when his truck broke down he wasn't paid until he had bought spare parts and paid for the repairs. Another of the wonders of the regime. Although he had his meals at the party cafeteria, our food became scarce. Occasionally I would go with him to the cafeteria, and the servers, thinking I must be Misha's little sister, gave me a meal, too. I guess I looked very young to them. Sometimes Misha was able to bring canned food or potatoes when he was on the road.

Cooking was another issue. I became friendly with the daughter who had returned from the kolkhoz and even played with her children. She gave me a small iron cooker that could stand on the edge of the stove above a space for firewood. I didn't have a pot, so the daughter gave me an old rusty Russian army mess tin, which was fairly deep and had a cover. That's what I used for cooking. We didn't have wood, so at night Misha and I would scavenge around the houses on our street and pull out planks of wooden fences. During the day I would chop the wood with an axe and make kindling. My diet consisted mostly of potatoes made in the cooker with some sauerkraut that I filched from the barrel in the kitchen.

One day, Misha came home with a large tin of pork that came from America. I decided to sell it and buy decent food instead. I went to the market and stood in a corner, holding the tin. I stood there for hours, but nobody seemed to notice me. People passed by and ignored me completely. Finally, a man approached me and said, "I'll buy the tin from you if you come eat with me." I thanked him but went home—with the tin of pork.

Another great difficulty was the freezing winter and my lack of warm clothing. Many of the stalls in the market sold woolen socks from Germany, apparently war booty that had found its way to the civilian population. I bought a few pairs of socks for next to nothing. I unraveled them and used the wool to knit gloves and sold the gloves at the market. Misha's light American jacket also underwent a transformation more suited to the Russian winter: Mrs. Ingeberg, the seamstress, sewed a lining of cotton wool for it. However, she ran out of material in the middle. The result was a jacket with a nice puffy lining at the top and limp fabric at the bottom.

Cash was a problem, too, so we decided to sell the ring Moshe Lichtenberg had given me. We went to a shop that had been recommended and showed the owner the ring. He examined it and shook his head.

"Sorry, but we don't have the clientele for a ring like this," he said.[4]

I remember two other events from around that time. The first was when Misha was transporting a library in his truck but three Russian books were left behind in one of the boxes. He brought them home and it proved an opportunity to teach myself Russian. It was a slow process and I took great pains reading, but I did it. I remember one was a book of poetry by the Ukrainian poet Shevchenko.[5] I even read stories in Russian to the children in the next room.

The second event was strange, alarming, and perhaps even symbolic, showing we were never going to be safe under Soviet rule. On those cold nights, I would bundle up as best I could and read to the light of a candle I had placed on the table near the window, which was a little below street level. One night, as I was sitting peacefully and reading, a drunken soldier took a shot at me and broke the silence of the night. First, I heard the shot, and then the sound of broken glass. I jumped up at once. The bullet had shattered the outside window and lodged in the frame between the outer and inner panes.

Winter's hold was relenting at last and spring was in the air. There were rumors that repatriation was approaching —the government was going to allow all foreign citizens to return to their native countries. This time when the NKVD officials came for their routine check, they told me in no uncertain terms that I had one week to register for repatriation, otherwise I would go to prison. I assumed that all the previous months that I had been allowed to remain there without working and registering were because they knew that foreigners would be repatriated. Now the time had come.

We'd certainly had enough of life in Minsk. And we knew that many of our friends were living in nearby Pinsk and were well settled and comfortable. So we decided to take a risk. Misha approached a clerk with whom he had become friendly at work and asked her to give him a travel permit for himself and his wife to travel to Pinsk. She agreed and Misha took the permit to his boss, who signed it without even looking at it.

That was it. We got up one morning, gathered our few belongings, and set off for Pinsk, intending never to return. We bought our tickets and boarded the train, knowing we could be considered deserters and might even be sent to Siberia if we were caught. We just hoped nobody would be looking for us since the repatriation had begun and Poles and Jews were starting to leave the Soviet Union on their way back to their country. Anyway, who cared whether another Polish Jew ran off and disappeared.

In Pinsk we felt truly free for the first time since the liberation. We reunited with many of our friends, all of whom had jobs and were living like human beings. One fellow we knew from Włodawa was David Tzinn. He was working as a dentist, although he was a dental technician by training, and doing well. He had government connections and helped others. Misha got a job right away as a driver for the health department and was happy with his work. We all lived in separate rooms in Tzinn's house: Avigdor and Rivka Shporrer, Andje, and Misha and I. As soon as we arrived, we hurried to register for repatriation, and Tzinn used his connections to speed up the process so that we could return to Poland as soon as possible.

Misha's mother had been born in Pinsk, so Misha immediately set out to look for relatives on his mother's side, the Tanzmans. His maternal grandfather ran a factory for matches in Pinsk and had six children: four daughters—Khassia (Misha's mother), Mina, Paula, and Fira (Esther, or Esfira in Russian)—and two sons—

Shmuel (Sam) and Meishl (Moshe). Shmuel had emigrated to America in the twenties and Khassia had married Yoseph Omelinski in Brest. When war broke out, Meishl escaped to Russia with Paula's husband and left his wife Tamar and small son Haim in Pinsk. All the others had remained in Pinsk.

Of that whole extended family, the only survivors in Pinsk itself were Fira, Tamar, and her son. After only a few days in Pinsk, Misha had found them and we were all thrilled. Misha had found a surviving aunt!

Their story of survival was heartbreaking. Fira had lost her husband, her parents and all her sisters in the roundup in which all the Jews in the city were murdered. The whole family had been hiding in a cellar, but the Germans had discovered it and ordered everyone to come out. They emerged one by one, but Tamar whispered to Fira to stay inside. Fira and her twelve-year-old son and Tamar and her three-year-old son stayed in the cellar, each hiding in a dark corner. They then managed to reach the house of a Polish acquaintance of Tamar's, who agreed to hide all four in his attic until the liberation. But then, sadly, Fira's son contracted tuberculosis and died shortly after the liberation.

I had hopes that Aunt Fira would be like a mother to me. They were quickly dashed. She was a simple and uneducated woman, spoke only Yiddish and a little Russian, and was almost illiterate. She loved clothes and the good life, but as for matters of the world, she was as helpless as a child and needed someone to take care of her.[6]

We continued ceaselessly to search for lost relatives as more and more survivors returned from Siberia and all sorts of hiding places, from the partisans and from the Red Army. A stunning, shocking reunion would await my husband.

* * *

Yitzele (Yitzhak) Friedman, a young man from Włodawa, was a partisan in the Kalinin otriad, and right after liberation was recruited to the Red Army. One day, while on leave, he came to stay with us in Pinsk. He had no surviving relatives and we were glad to have him. To entertain him, we decided to take him to a movie. I even remember which one it was: *Six Hours after the War*, a Soviet war film that was so popular that tickets were hard to get. As we were leaving the cinema, Yitzele realized his wallet had been stolen with all his documents. He immediately reported the theft to the police and was issued temporary papers.

A few days later we realized this was a good opportunity to free Yitzele from the Red Army. A young Russian woman named Suzanna, who was in love with Tzinn, forged a travel permit to Brest for Yitzele and stamped it with her father's official stamp (he was a general and military governor of the city). Yitzele was able to leave the city in civilian dress, travel to Brest, cross the border to Poland, and then make it all the way to Italy and, finally, Palestine.[7]

Not long after Yitzele had defected and disappeared, however, we received notice from the police that someone named Private Friedman should claim his lost documents. This was a new problem: what would happen if the police found out Yitzele had disappeared? But this, too, proved an opportunity to get someone out of Pinsk.

Another acquaintance of ours, Nakhum Knopfmacher, who bore enough of a resemblance to Yitzele, went to the station, declared he was Friedman and collected the documents. Now he had a soldier's documents; all he needed was a travel permit. Suzanna again came to our aid. Using her father's official stamp, she validated a new travel permit for another soldier named Friedman. Nakhum was now free to search for his own relatives. Thus Nakhum, in army uniform, made his way to Brest.

Of the nearly twenty-five thousand Jews who were trapped in Brest-Litovsk on the day the Germans invaded, fewer than twenty were left in town after the war. Survivors who were searching for people would gather at the house of the Katsov sisters. That's where Nakhum Knopfmacher went, too. Suddenly the door opened and two Soviet Jewish officers burst in. One of them started to interrogate Nakhum and all the other survivors. Nakhum couldn't take his eyes off the officer—he looked so familiar, but he couldn't remember who he was. Finally Nakhum turned to him and asked, "Is it possible we know each other?"

The officer looked at him and said, "I don't think so."

"What's your name?" Nakhum asked.

"Omelinski," the officer replied.

"Really?" said Nakhum, "I know a fellow by that name, Misha Omelinski."

The officer jumped up excitedly. "What?! That's my brother!"

"He is in Pinsk now," said Nakhum, And he has a wife."

And so, Misha's older brother Soleh (Ysrael) found out that Misha was alive.

Both brothers had been avid athletes, and when the Soviets entered Brest in September 1939, Soleh declared that he was a sports instructor and was sent as a coach to another town. It turned out that in 1941, when the Germans invaded the Soviet Union, Soleh was drafted into the Red Army—at the time he had already joined the Communist Party. Because he was an outstanding soldier, he was eventually promoted and reached the rank of lieutenant. He spent the whole war in the Red Army and in April 1945 reached Berlin with his unit.

Since he was talented and proficient in several languages, his commanders offered to send him to the Soviet school for diplomats in Leningrad, so he went, accompanied by another officer. The two were traveling on one permit and were expected to report for duty in Moscow and, from there, travel to Leningrad. On their way to Moscow, Soleh suggested stopping in Brest to look for relatives, and that's when he ran into Nakhum and discovered Misha was alive.

Soleh convinced his friend to go to Pinsk with him to search for Misha, and the next day they continued by train. When they reached Pinsk, Soleh said goodbye to his friend and started to make inquiries until he found a Jew who said, "I know Omelinski. I'll take you to him."

It was dusk, almost evening. It got dark quickly. Misha and I were taking a walk—I don't remember where and why—and there, coming toward us, were a tall Soviet officer, and next to him a man in civilian clothes. Misha was deep in thought, but I glanced at the officer's face as we passed by and froze. "Misha," I said, "look at that man. Who is he?"

Misha stopped and looked up and the officer turned to look at us.

"Soleh!" Misha shouted, and the two brothers fell into each other's arms.

* * *

Soleh stayed with us for a day or two and we got to know each other. We shared our stories and adjusted to the thought that Misha had a brother and I a brother-in-law. Then Soleh had to be on his way to Moscow.

Soleh Omelinski

The process of repatriation went quickly. David Tzinn, Andje, and Rivka and Avigdor Shporrer packed all their belongings and went to Włodawa. They were driven to the train station in the governor's official car thanks to the loyal Suzanna. The following week, Misha and I went to Brest-Litovsk.

A Jewish man who had been a partisan in north Belorussia allowed us use of a room in his house. Misha wandered the streets of the city in search of remnants of his past. Meanwhile we received a date for our repatriation. Suddenly, the thought of going home was a reality.

I was overwhelmed with tremendous feelings of homesickness. Memories came back in waves: the house, the courtyard, the streets, my family, friends, and everyone I had ever known in my short life. And all those I knew I would never see again. Deep in my heart I hoped beyond reason that someone had survived. Maybe my little sister Khumka?

One night after midnight, I awoke to the sound of shooting. The blast was so loud and sounded so near I was sure it was anti-aircraft fire and that we would be bombed. But how could that be? The war was being fought in Berlin. We quickly dressed and went outside.

The streets were full of people: crowds of Russians, Belorussians, Poles, Jews, young and old—in short, the whole city. They were all cheering and rejoicing, dancing and hugging. Anyone who had a firearm fired like crazy into the air.

Nazi Germany had surrendered. The war in Europe was over. The date was May 9, 1945.

At last, the day we had been waiting for came. About two weeks after we had arrived at Brest, we boarded the train and were on our way back home. The train crossed the border at Terespol, on the Bug River across from Brest-Litovsk, turned southward to Chelm, and then continued north to the Włodawa Orchówek station. At the station, we rented a cart and drove it to town. With growing excitement and anticipation, we rolled slowly down the familiar streets until we reached the compound.

A young girl was standing at the entrance. It was one of the neighbors' daughters, Stashka. She was wearing a dress of dark blue chiffon with white polka dots, which I remembered with painful longing—the dress I had worn at Aunt Eva's wedding. Mama and I had chosen the fabric. Yidiska had said it brought out the blue in my eyes.

I pointed to her and my voice was loud and rather decisive. "That's my dress," I said.

"No, it isn't. My aunt gave it to me," said the girl.

I repeated, this time more aggressively, "It's my dress!"

The girl ran off and we went into the compound.[8]

The familiar sound of the electric power station welcomed us. The flour mill was also operating. The courtyard was full of people and carts. The house at the entrance seemed whole but deserted. Grandpa Shaya's house looked the same. Our house, however, stood in ruins, with a huge gap in the roof.

Our former friends and neighbors congregated around us in the yard and everyone was asking questions. Moshe Spokoyne, one of grandpa's partners, and his son Moniek had come out of hiding in the village of Wyryki and were living in grandpa's house and running the whole business. I introduced Misha: "This is my husband Misha, from Brest-Litovsk."

"Is he a good husband?" asked Kovalchik, one of the Polish neighbors.

"As good as my father," I said.

At that moment, our old mechanic Kaminski came out of the power station and looked at me incredulously. "You're alive," he exclaimed.

He ran toward me shouting, and then kneeled and kissed my hands.

We both cried tears of joy.

There was one more surprise waiting for us in Włodawa: Soleh was there waiting for us. He had gone to Moscow with his friend and received a travel permit for Leningrad. But on an impulse, he had decided he wanted to join his brother and go west and leave the Soviet Union. The next day, he arrived at the station, but the train had left. His friend, and the travel permit, were on their way to Leningrad. Soleh soon was arrested. He was demoted, his head was shaved, and were it not for his glorious past service record, he probably would have faced a long prison term in the gulag.

Instead he was attached to a penal battalion and sent to the west. When the train was near Włodawa, he jumped off and escaped.

Survivors in Włodawa, 1945, by the canal dug by Jewish forced laborers (Misha and I on the right)

Slowly the survivors from Włodawa were returning home. Partisans returned from the forests. Those who had escaped east before the war, those who had deserted, and those who had been hiding in homes of non-Jews—all of them came back to town and started to look for friends and relatives.

We stayed with Spokoyne and his son in Grandpa Shaya's house. The power station and the flour mill were not only operating but lucrative. We received our share of the proceeds and didn't need to work. We spent our time wandering the streets, taking photos, visiting friends, and playing cards like people of leisure. The town looked pretty much the same as before, aside from the work camp and closed ghetto, which stood in ruins like an ugly scar in the middle of the town. The synagogue, which the Nazis had used to store grain during the occupation, had not been damaged. The holy ark had not been touched. Even the mayor, Alexander Behr, who had been replaced, came back and was happy to see us. That was when we went to look for the treasure that my father had buried at the Mandels', only to find it empty.

We dreamed, as did all the survivors, of giving a proper Jewish burial to all those who had been murdered in Adampol and in other villages. But then we met Isaac Rothenberg in Włodawa, and when we heard his horrifying story, we understood the dream was not to be.

Rothenberg had been sent to Sobibor in one of the roundups, but he and his brother had not been sent to the gas chamber. In October 1943, a prisoners' revolt broke out,[9] and Isaac and his brother managed to escape to the nearby forests. Isaac lost his brother there and eventually was captured by local Poles and turned over, along with another Jewish fellow, to Zelinger, the Nazi in charge of the Adampol villages.

Zelinger held the two men captive in a stable, chained like dogs, and exhibited them to his guests. Then the two were attached to a team of Jews in forced labor, whose job was to hide evidence of the murders that had taken place. They removed corpses from mass graves in the area of Adampol and burned them in large bonfires. Eventually Rothenberg managed to escape and reached Greenspan's partisan group.[10]

It took some time, but we eventually realized that we had no future in Włodawa. Even our murdered loved ones were not buried here. And antisemitism was becoming more widespread and dangerous all over Poland. Although we were permitted to carry a weapon, we did not feel safe. Meanwhile, vast territories of eastern Germany, as well as all the German cities that had previously belonged to Poland, had been annexed to Poland and the German inhabitants had been expelled. The Polish government was encouraging all refugees who had no place to go to settle in areas formerly occupied by Germans, so it presented an opportunity to move on.

We spent all of that summer in Włodawa. Life was comfortable. We took long walks in the town, in what remained of the ghetto ruins, and along the canal that the forced laborers had dug. And we took lots of photos.

When I look at the photos from those days, I don't see Holocaust refugees broken in body and spirit. I see a group of handsome and healthy young people, well dressed and smiling. It is a wonder how, after all we had been through, that we could look forward into the future. But we were young, and maybe that explains everything.

They didn't break us. After all, we had a future.

Sara and Misha Omelinski, 1946

Knowing we had no future in Poland, in the fall of 1945 we rented out the whole compound and sold Uncle Itche's house for three hundred dollars. We packed our belongings and went to Szczecin (formerly the German city Stettin) on the Baltic Sea. We lived in one of the apartments of Germans who had been expelled and made our living working at a business that had been left behind. In January 1946, in the apartment in Szczecin, I gave birth to our eldest daughter, Batya, named after my mother.

But we knew we had to get out of the Soviet bloc. We decided to make our escape into the American-occupied zone of Germany. Three months later, in the middle of the night, I crossed the border with my infant by hiding in a military truck full of Soviet soldiers. When the truck reached the checkpoint, the baby started to cry. All the soldiers suddenly started singing at full volume, so we were able to cross without being detected. Misha followed us a week later in a mail truck.

We were integrated into a United Nations Relief and Rehabilitation Administration camp for displaced persons in the American section of Berlin and lived there for some time. However, two months or so later, the camp was moved to a new location in Bavaria because of growing animosity between the Americans and the Soviets. We received lodgings in Gabersee, which had been a village for the mentally ill, not far from Munich. Hitler had eliminated its inhabitants as part of his infamous "Euthanasia Program", the mass murder of the disabled and mentally ill. In June 1948, our son Yossi (Joseph David, after both our fathers) was born in Wasserburg am Inn, an adjacent town.

Uncle Weller sent us immigration papers (affidavits) from America and even arranged an apartment for us in New York, but we decided to go to Israel instead. In 1948, when the state of Israel was declared, we sailed for Israel on the *Galila*.

---

1. Originally Hebrew, meaning "your people," usually used in the sense of "one of us."
2. The Soviet secret police before the KGB.
3. We had a Jewish ceremony two years later in the displaced persons' camp in Germany.
4. We finally sold it to pay for the release of our belongings from customs when we emigrated to Israel.
5. Shevchenko was the national poet of the Ukraine (1814–61), renowned for his folk poetry and his drawings.
6. Fira attempted to emigrate to Palestine on the Exodus, but along with all the other illegal émigrés was sent back to Germany. She finally emigrated after Israel became a state. She lived in Ramat Gan and died at a ripe old age.
7. Yitzhak (Yitzele) Friedman joined the anti-British underground in Palestine and was commended for his participation in action. He was killed in 1948 in an attack against the British at Pardes Hana.
8. Sometime afterward, we visited Stashka's house and, in addition to the dress, we found other objects belonging to us. We took all of them back.

9. There were numerous attempts to escape from Sobibor, and the Germans retaliated by killing dozens of prisoners. The revolt broke out on October 14, 1943 and about three hundred prisoners escaped. Following the revolt, the Germans liquidated the camp.
10. Rothenberg emigrated to Israel. In 1994 he was murdered by two Palestinian terrorists who worked at the building site where he was the foreman.

EPILOGUE

Our story would not be complete without mentioning what became of one man who tried to help the Jews of Włodawa and others who were complicit in the Nazi war crimes.

Even after the last roundup, as noted earlier, Bernhard Falkenberg, the German who saved hundreds of Jews from Włodawa, tried as best he could to save more of the town's Jews. He remained in contact with Lichtenberg's partisan group when they were first getting started and supplied them with money, food, medications, and more. In the summer of 1943, when the go-between Kozlovski was caught, Falkenberg was arrested, too, tried, and sent to Mauthausen concentration camp in Austria. He was released when the allies liberated the camp in 1945. Falkenberg lived in East Germany after the war, not far from Berlin, and in the summer of 1964 he testified in the trial against war criminals of Włodawa. Some of the Jewish witnesses even met him at the court. He died in 1966, and three years later, in 1969, Yad Vashem posthumously awarded him the honor of "Righteous Gentile."

As for the Nazi war criminals who were active in Włodawa, in the summer of 1964, a trial was held in Hanover against a number of those S.D. men, including Richard Nitschke, Anton Miller, Josef Schmidt, Adolf Schaub, and others. They were accused of having transported thousands of Jews to Sobibor and of having murdered POWs, Jews, and Poles. I was honored to have been one of the survivors of Włodawa who was called to testify in that trial. Other witnesses–Falkenberg was one of them–came from many countries worldwide. I mainly testified regarding the murder of the Rabbi of Radzyń, as I was an eye witness. The accused were sentenced to prison terms of two to five years.

In August 1972, I was summoned again, this time to Hamburg, in the trial against Germans who trained the Ukrainians and the Belorussian (at Travniki) to aid them in the extermination. In my testimony, I was asked to describe the behavior of the "Blacks" during the roundups.

TESTIMONY OF MISHA OMELINSKI

In 1998, about two years before my father's death, I finally decided to interview him and record the stories he used to tell me for as long as I can remember. I was hoping to record it all in an organized fashion, so clearly and in such detail that it would present a broad and reliable picture of his experiences during the Holocaust.[1] I knew before I started that it would not be easy for either of us. But the Holocaust was so central a period of his life that I believed we would succeed.

He was eighty-two and had not yet been diagnosed with the cancer that would kill him two years later. I interviewed him with my mother four or five times, for about two hours each time, in their flat in Givatayim. He related his story fluently and without hesitation, even though he had forgotten a number of details, names, and dates. But aside from the events themselves, I was unable to get him to describe much or share feelings, and there were certain personal events he categorically refused to talk about.

The result is this document, which might best be described as a testimony. It is unembellished and straightforward, the story exactly as he told it, no more and no less—a faithful reflection of the man himself.

- Yossi Millo

Misha, 1936

I was born Michael (Misha) Omelinski,[2] son of Yossef and Khassia, in Brisk (Brest-Litovsk, then Poland) in 1916. My father owned a pharmacy on the main street of the city. I had four brothers: Yisrael (Soleh) was the eldest, and Nathan, Eliezer (Lollek), and Aharon were younger than me. I finished elementary school and then went to the Maslovski Gymnasium but didn't graduate. From 1937 to 1939 I served in the Polish army. During that time, I was trained as a medic, and having been promoted to corporal, I was stationed at the regional military hospital in the Brest Fortress, where I was made head of the emergency room. After being released from the army, Soleh and I opened a cosmetics shop. In my free time I played soccer in the city's Jewish sports club, and even became a local celebrity.

Then in 1939, World War II broke out and I was drafted again to the Polish army. After just twenty-eight days my unit was surrounded by the Germans near the city of Dęblin and surrendered. The Germans locked the whole company inside the town synagogue, but on the first night, taking advantage of the general chaos, I managed to climb out through a window and escape with another soldier, a Pole. I even had my gun on me. We walked east and several days later crossed the Bug River shortly before the bridge was blown up, arriving safely in Brisk.

By then, the city was already under Soviet control. Right after the Soviets got control of the city, they closed down all the Jewish institutions and deported east those inhabitants whom they considered "enemies of the workers' class." That was how my parents received identity papers requiring them to live at least one hundred kilometers from the border and had to leave Brisk and move east. They set out with my three younger brothers—Nathan, Lollek, and Aharon (Soleh was in another city working as a sports instructor). However, they managed—probably by bribing someone—to settle in Kobryn, a town near Brest-Litovsk and only less than fifty kilometers from the Bug, the new Polish border. When I reported to the government officials, I claimed that I was a professional driver, and so I got an identity document allowing me to remain in Brisk, a Soviet driver's license, and a job with a company that delivered food and clothing to the army. My boss was a Jewish Soviet senior officer named Gorelik, a nice, easygoing guy. I am not sure whether he knew I was Jewish, but I knew he was. I was assigned to stay with a family living on Kościuszko Boulevard and shared a room with a fellow named Yankl, from Międzyrzec Podlaski.

One day, Gorelik approached me and instructed me to load a barrel of oil and all the gasoline from the garage onto the car. He then asked for my address and told me not to leave the house. I did what he asked, but even then I did not suspect that war was about to break out again. No one suspected the Germans were going to invade the USSR. There were no signs.

* * *

On June 22, 1941, at 2 a.m., I woke up in a panic. The walls and the window panes were shaking. Brest-Litovsk was being bombed! We dressed quickly and hurried out, but near the gate we had to run for cover and lie down— bombs were falling on the city with furious frequency. We saw soldiers running out of the fortress in their underwear, clutching their trousers as they ran. At dawn, the gates of the massive city prison opened, and crowds of prisoners emerged and scattered about. An ungodly riot erupted in the city and masses started looting the shops, particularly for food and alcohol.

A short time after sunrise, at about 7 a.m., rumors reached us that the Germans had crossed the Mukhavets River and were advancing. Soon there were German soldiers everywhere, and many settled on the boulevard where we lived. We approached and they called to us, handed us a bucket, and ordered us to bring them water. They used the water to wash up and in return gave us cigarettes. They treated us as soldiers would treat nonhostile civilians—they didn't ask who was Jewish and who not, and basically didn't show much interest in us.

But a few days later, notices went up instructing all the Jews to report to the labor office to be assigned work.

When we got there, we found a German waiting for workers, but we were the only ones—nobody else had the guts. Yankl and I were taken to the Adria Cinema, given rakes, and ordered to clean a large dumpster. When the lunch break came and the Germans all went to eat, we dumped the rakes, jumped over the fence, and ran back home. The following morning we reported to the labor office again, and this time a German officer was waiting outside. He called aloud, "Come! Come here!" and took us to a large elementary school. We were ordered to get rid of everything inside. "This is going to be a hospital for wounded German soldiers," he said.

We worked hard, emptying out all the desks and benches and army mattresses into the schoolyard, and at 11 o'clock the officer told us to take a break. He went and brought us lunch—a nutritious meal including meat—and told us to come back the next day and bring five more "strong fellows" like ourselves.

We did just that and continued to empty out the school and get it cleaned up. Once the building was ready, it was turned into a hospital, and a stream of wounded soldiers from the front started to flow in. Only Yankl and I were kept on to work, mostly in the yard, where the wounded were triaged before being admitted.

Five or six days after the Germans arrived, they started to round up Jews for "work." About five thousand of the strongest and most robust Jewish men were rounded up, all those between the ages of seventeen and forty. On that particular day, Yankl and I had gone for a swim in the river. On the beach were a few young gentiles, and I noticed that they were whispering among themselves. Then I overheard one of them say, as they got ready to leave, "Hey Ántek, let's go. They're rounding up all the Jews."

We got dressed in a hurry and rushed back to town. There we saw a convoy of trucks full of Jews. We walked at leisure and didn't give it much thought. When we got home, the landlady was beside herself.

"Good grief, I was so worried," she said. "What are you doing here? All the Jews are being sent to work."

I told Yankl I thought we should try to catch up with the convoy. "We don't want to be left here alone, right?" I said.

So we ran out and followed the trucks, which were already on their way out of the city, but a German soldier stopped us and ordered us back.

"Never mind!" we consoled each other. "If they want us, they know where to find us."

The five thousand Jews who were taken that day were never heard from again. Only sometime later did we learn about the massacre: they had been driven to the outskirts of the city, a place called Kotelnia, near a brick factory, and shot.

* * *

One day in October or November 1941, about five months after the German occupation, instructions were posted about the creation of a ghetto. At about the same time, the Jews were ordered to replace the armband with a yellow star to be worn on the chest and on the back. I had a pass enabling me free movement in and out of the ghetto because of my work for the Germans in the hospital, but I hardly went to the ghetto, preferring to stay at the hospital day and night. In the ghetto, conditions were terrible, with thirty thousand Jews—six thousand of them from the surrounding villages.

In mid-December, the ghetto was closed. Actually, there were two ghettos in Brest-Litovsk, the large ghetto and the small ghetto, with the main road to the east, to Belorussia and the Soviet Union, separating them. By that time, conditions had worsened. People had literally begun to starve. Also at that time, a Jewish police force was created. The Judenrat had been in existence earlier, since August 1941.

And then there was a chance encounter. At the hospital, large vats for disinfection were installed in the yard, and extra Jewish workers from the ghetto were sent to help with the disinfection. A few of them had connections with the underground, which, as it turned out, was already active in the Brisk ghetto. The underground had been operating under the auspices of left-wing organizations founded by Jewish communists from Russia. Two of those workers became friendly with me—Yankl Fuchs and another fellow whose name I don't remember—and at the time I had no idea what they wanted from me. Finally, one of them passed me a note on the sly, "They're waiting for you in the ghetto."

I joined him and followed him into the ghetto, through back alleys, openings in fences, into a house, and down unlit stairs that led to a dark cellar. Three men were seated at a table, a candle for light, and one of them addressed me:

"Comrade Omelinski," he said, "all factions have now joined together as one and established an underground. Our aim is to save the Jews who are still alive."

In short, they had heard I was a veteran of the Polish army and wanted me to join and be in charge of arms collection. I immediately agreed.

The underground was composed of secret cells of three members each. I was appointed head of one of the cells. Communication between the cells was through a "connector," a go-between who knew the heads of three cells. Our connector was Fischel, a carter by trade and a petty criminal. When I met him sometime later, he suggested that I get work at the fortress as there were plenty of weapons and some of our people were already working there. At that time I was already working at the fortress on occasion, chopping down hay to fill mattresses for the hospital. I understood it was not a suggestion but rather an order, and I accepted at once even though I was happy working at the hospital.

The fortress of Brest-Litovsk had fallen to the Germans only six months after they occupied the city, when the front had almost reached Moscow.[3] The defenders were Uzbek and Tartar soldiers who held on bravely and didn't surrender despite the murderous air and ground bombardment. The fortress walls were six or seven meters thick and the bombs didn't destroy them. During the battle for the fortress, the Germans would use Jews in order to remove their dead and wounded from the battlefield. The fortress finally fell to the Germans and all its defenders got killed.

The sights inside the fortress were appalling and horrendous. There were four-barrel anti-aircraft guns with half-burned bodies of their operators still seated on them. But we had to get used to those horrors and focus on getting weapons. And there were plenty. The challenge was to smuggle them out. Each worker was checked upon entering and exiting the fortress. And when exiting, we had to march in groups in the middle of the street. No one was allowed to bend down, not even to pick up a cigarette stub—anyone who bent down or walked on the sidewalk risked being shot. Despite the restrictions we did manage to smuggle weapons out, and then to spirit them into the ghetto. Fellows swam across the river—the fortress had been built on an island formed by the meeting of the Mukhavets and Bug rivers—and they dragged the weapons across on makeshift rafts to where other teams were waiting to receive them. Other resistance members worked at the Soviet military airfield, where they removed guns of smashed and burned aircraft and smuggled them in pieces into the ghetto. Those operations were complicated and required daring and courage, but as far as I recall no one was caught in the act. In any case, it wasn't long before quite a sizable arsenal was accumulated in the ghetto. I was put in charge of a number of machine guns because I was familiar with weapons of that sort from my army service.

A Russian Jew by the name of Ochsenboim, who had been the city's nominee for office in the Supreme Soviet of the Republic during Soviet reign, explained the underground's plan: we will work in squads, and each squad will be equipped with a machine gun. When the Germans attempt to liquidate the ghetto (there were rumors that the liquidation was being planned), some of the groups will set fire to the ghetto while others will open fire, and all the Jews—men, women and children—will have to run in one direction—through Kobrynska and Jagiellonska Streets—to the forests. Members of the underground will follow and shoot and throw grenades at the enemy. Some will make it, some will not, but no one will be herded onto the trucks.

And so I carried on working at the fortress. I would deliver weapons to those whose job it was to disassemble them and hide the pieces. One day during breakfast, I suddenly noticed a Belgian pistol just lying there on the ground at my feet. Even though I felt panic and was afraid it might be a trap, I covered the pistol with one of the two bricks I had been sitting on. But no one seemed to notice, what with so many guns scattered about. After work, I took the pistol with me and brought it to the ghetto, where someone cleaned it and returned it to me. I don't remember what happened to it after that. Meanwhile the amounts of weapons and ammunition that had accumulated in the ghetto were such that we were instructed not to bring small amounts of bullets, but whole crates only. At that point I asked to go back to work at the hospital.

Mojżesz (Misha) Omelinski, application form, Brest Ghetto, circa 1942

My main job at the hospital was to take care of the central heating system, but I did other jobs as well. The German patients had no idea I was Jewish. Once, while I was busy putting blackout shades on the windows, one of the injured soldiers asked me where in Germany I came from. Another fellow, a German officer from Bavaria, took me under his wing: his name was Aushield, and I remember him as a kind-hearted man.

One day while we were chatting, I asked him a direct question: "What would you do if the Germans liquidated the ghetto and I hid here?"

"I would turn a blind eye," he answered.

And I believe he would have. At the same time, they started to bring in Soviet prisoners from a large POW camp that had been set up right across from the hospital, once the site of a church and a government office building. The hospital would request ten or fifteen prisoners to work in maintenance, and at 4 p.m. would escort them back to their camp. My relationship with Aushield was so good that he would sometimes give me his rifle and tell me to bring the prisoners to work. I would hang the rifle on my shoulder, go into the POW camp, and shout, "Ten workers—come on—march." And I would lead them to work. During their breaks, some of the workers would come to the furnace room to warm up.

Some Soviet prisoners, mostly officers, became my friends and trusted me. One day, one of them confided in me that they were looking for a way to escape into the forest. We started to cook up escape plans—all sorts of crazy ideas came up like hijacking a truck and driving it out of the city. But nothing came of those plans. Finally, I suggested that the Russians wait until the underground gave the word, and the prisoners could be smuggled into the ghetto, and from there to the forests. The prisoners agreed; they had no other choice.

Meanwhile we heard about a Russian officer who had been imprisoned in the fortress but found shelter in the ghetto. Someone snitched and the officer was found and executed. The informer, a Jewish policeman from Warsaw, was subsequently attacked by members of the underground. He had been invited to meet a woman, and there the trap had been laid. Two fellows, Ochsenboim and Kagan, stabbed him. The man was brought to the hospital and, despite his injuries, managed to blurt out the name Kagan. Kagan was therefore forced to flee, and he found shelter in the attic of the ghetto pharmacy. In order to silence the injured policeman, the underground instructed one of the Jewish doctors at the hospital to eliminate him. I heard this story from Ochsenboim himself, and although I never told the Russian prisoners, it was now clear that it would be impossible to smuggle them into the ghetto.

Throughout that period, I hardly lived in the ghetto and I knew little of what was happening there. Meanwhile rumors were spreading about the liquidation of ghettos in all sorts of places. Frightened and alarmed refugees were pouring in from Domachevo and Kobryn, but you couldn't get them to talk. My father also arrived from Kobryn and told us what had happened there. Fear was very much in the air. The Judenrat was summoned to the Gestapo and ordered to pay an enormous ransom of money, gold, and other valuables. The demands increased over time and were so high that it was impossible to meet them. Nerves were more and more on edge.

One day, an S.S. unit responsible for the liquidation of ghettos in the area entered the city. The Germans convened the local police forces (Poles and Ukrainians) with their own forces in the large Shviat Cinema, where a speaker instructed the forces. Members of the Polish underground were present, and through them the information reached our underground. Apparently the S.S. had informed the police forces what to do once the decision was made to liquidate the ghetto.

That same day, I received a note telling me in no uncertain terms to go back to the ghetto and stay there every night from then on. The ghetto underground was ready to rebel, and all units were on alert. Machine guns were assembled and positioned, which was no easy task as the heavy machine guns had no tripods and we had to improvise, sticking them in walls or steadying them in any way possible. Thus, we had six or seven heavy machine guns ready. And then a dispute broke out in the ghetto: many ghetto residents implored the underground to take no action and not give the Germans an excuse to liquidate the ghetto.

But after the assembly at the cinema, the S.S. unit left the city and moved on to Kobryn. In retrospect I think it must have been a diversionary tactic. I have no doubt that the Germans had precise information about the underground, from informants in the ghetto, because on the day of the liquidation they immediately encircled the central bunker, where some fifty people were stationed with arms and radio equipment and blew it up.

A few days passed and life in the ghetto slowly went back to normal. People went back to their activities, their families, and their worries. The underground leaders instructed their men to stay alert, but their orders went unheeded. It was during the fall of 1942, sometime after Yom Kippur. I had returned to the ghetto very early that morning to sleep. To my surprise I saw a motorcycle with three German soldiers on it, in helmets and full gear, entering the ghetto and riding toward the ghetto police station. I went there, too, because I knew the head of police, but the policemen on duty shouted at me and wouldn't let me in even though I told them I wanted to report a break-in.

I was heading toward the small ghetto and had not even crossed the main road when Peska Shedletski, the violinist, came running and shouting in alarm, "Misha, the cars have returned from Kobryn! They are surrounding the ghetto!"

The picture was clear: dozens of vehicles had taken positions around the ghetto at set intervals of twenty to thirty meters apart. Men had gotten out and were stationed all along the fence. Here and there were armored vehicles. I immediately turned back and ran toward the central bunker. By this time, the ghetto was completely encircled, and minutes later, the armored vehicles drove through, trampled the fence with their wheels, took positions at intersections, and fired furiously into the streets.

It was a complete surprise. It was immediately clear that members of the underground were cut off from the posts they were supposed to man, and there was no way they could reach them. Total chaos broke out instantly and people were running in the streets in a panic. Germans were shooting indiscriminately. I, too, ran through the streets with everyone. It was getting lighter and bursts of gunfire could be heard everywhere. I finally found a place to hide under the floor of a house—I pulled out a few loose bricks and climbed into the gap between the foundations and the floor. Seconds later, six or seven people crawled in after me, and we then replaced the loose bricks from the inside. Through the cracks I could see people being herded toward the main street, and from there onto waiting trucks. The day wore on. The sun kept rising in the sky. And all that day people were being marched on and on.

With evening and darkness, things became quiet, but still we stayed in the hiding place. We sat there for four days and five nights, with no food and no water. On the third day, five black-shirted Ukrainians came toward the house. They stopped near our hiding place, and one of them kicked the bricks, which fell inside. I was lying near the opening, and my heart was beating so wildly I was sure they could hear it.

"There's no one in there," said one of them in Russian.

"Try anyway," said another.

A moment later, the barrel of a rifle was pushing through. With extreme effort, I managed to move my leg parallel to the barrel so as not to be hit. I braced myself for the shot. When it came, it was like thunder in that closed space. No one made a sound. No one even breathed. The Ukrainians left and we never moved the bricks back in place.

On the fifth night, we decided to go out. To tell the truth, I was afraid, but a young guy convinced me to go with him, and he climbed out first. The moment I got out, my head started spinning—most likely because of hunger pangs and the clear air outside—and I fell. I leaned against the wall until I felt better, and the youngster held on to me as we walked. We went into the adjacent house, which belonged to a well-known surgeon, Dr. Sarnaker. On the window sill, we found a dirty jar with some jam in it, and in the kitchen some dry bread and moldy sausage. We ate all of it ravenously and wandered on.

Everywhere we went, you could see devastating sights of what had happened. In one of the houses, a long ladder stood against the wall from the ground to the attic, and the battered and smashed body of a young girl lay nearby. We went into other houses, changed clothes, and carried as much as we could back to the hiding place.

We told the others what we had seen and decided we would all leave the next night. I asked and found out that two of us were members of the underground who knew where the remaining weapons—those that had not been assigned to the squads—were hidden. Those two said they would go out and get the weapons while the others would forage for food. We would then meet and decide how to get out of the ghetto and escape to the forests.

The following night, the two underground members came back with three rifles and a large supply of ammunition and grenades. There were also three machine guns that the men had wrapped in sacks and left outside the house where the weapons had been hidden. We could take them with us later. We organized a little food and checked out the area. Police cars were patrolling the ghetto during the day, but at night they left. We decided we would leave from Kościuszko Street, where a wide ditch ran along the border of the ghetto.

The following night, we packed the little food we had, wrapped the weapons in sacks and scraps of cloth, and were on our way. By this time, our group numbered thirteen, including four or five women. As planned, we went to where the machine guns were supposed to be, but they were gone. The Germans must have found them.

"In that case," I said, "they must be waiting for us. Let's get out of here."

We continued toward the edge of the ghetto, near the train station hospital on Kobryńska Street. We didn't see a soul.

There was a high barbed wire fence along which guards were patrolling. Two pairs of guards marched toward each other, and in passing marched to the end of their route, and then turned and marched back. We agreed that each time the guards walked away, one of us would crawl under the barbed wire and wait in the alley on the other side. Three of us escaped with no incident, but the fourth got stuck as his clothes snagged the wire. The rustle alerted the guards and one of them hurried back, looked for a few moments, and then continued patrolling. A few more of our group managed to crawl through, but then another got stuck, panicked, and ran back. This time the guards saw him, and one of them started walking toward where we were hiding. There was no way out.

I said to my friends, "Listen, I was in the army and I should have no problem shooting a person standing eight meters away. Let me load one rifle, then one of you will go and try to bribe the guard. If it doesn't work, I'll shoot him."

Sonya Greenspan walked toward the guard and we soon saw her slip something into his hand. I stayed behind with one other fellow while the others went out and quickly crossed the fence.

I handed the rifle to the other fellow and said, "I will go talk to the guard. Try to cross over with the rifle."

I went up to the guard and said, "My dear friend, you seem to be a nice person. Why don't you let me give you a little souvenir?"

He answered me in broken Polish, "Watches."

Very slowly I removed the watch from my wrist and handed it to him. When I saw that the fellow with the rifle had crossed over, I thanked the guard and crossed over, too.

Now we were outside the ghetto, on Krótka Street, and walked toward Jagiellonska Street. From there we needed to pass close to the slaughterhouse and on to the bridge over the Mukhavets River, on the road to Domachevo, and from there to the Polygon (previously an army camp). On Jagiellonska Street we ran into a patrol of six Germans. In the black of night and in dead silence, we walked past and they didn't bother us. They probably never imagined that Jews would be wandering about like that. Soon we reached the bridge.

According to underground intelligence reports, the bridge was not guarded, but guards were probably stationed there after the liquidation of the ghetto. Nevertheless, we thought it best to find out, so I scouted the area with one other fellow. The bridge was fairly long, about sixty meters, and slightly curved. On the farther end we suddenly came upon a blue and white striped hut. Inside, a German soldier seemed to be nodding off. I froze. My eyes were glued to him in a complete panic. If only I had known then what later experience taught me, I would surely have known what to do. Suddenly the German woke up, alarmed—maybe he felt I was staring at him—grabbed his rifle and shouted in German, "Hands up!"

We stood and raised our arms.

"Who are you? Are you Jews?" asked the German.

"We are Poles," I answered. "We were at a wedding in the city and now we're on our way home."

But he ordered us to wait there until his replacement came. The fellow with me, who was very brave, suggested we attack him, but I said we should wait and see. Meanwhile the rest of our group were waiting at the other end of the bridge, and when they didn't receive the agreed-upon okay signal, they sent another guy to check it out. That person got as close as where the bridge curved and then stopped. The guard noticed him and shot at him but missed, and the fellow ran back.

"Must be a Jew," the German muttered.

To support the claim that we were Poles, I suggested—in Polish and using gestures—that I would go back and get the Jew.

"Okay, go get him," said the guard, "but your friend will stay here till you get back."

I walked off slowly and cautiously, constantly looking behind me. The shot would no doubt have alerted the Germans and more troops would be sent shortly. Or might the guard shoot me in the back? I took longer strides and reached the group.

What do we do now? We could try to free our friend, or we could run off. We contemplated some crazy ideas, like swimming under the bridge across the river and throwing a grenade into the guard's hut. But we dismissed all these plans as there was not enough time and dawn would soon be breaking. I tried to convince the others to all go back and overpower the guard. He couldn't shoot all of us with one rifle, could he? The others argued that he had shot once, so he would shoot again, and anyway twenty minutes had passed and the reinforcement would surely be coming any minute. In the end, it was decided to leave our friend to his fate and get away. What choice did we have?

So we turned right and walked along the Mukhavets to a spot where boats were anchored, hoping to find a place to cross. When we reached the place, called Pogon, it was starting to get light, so we found a place to hide under the boathouse floorboards and stayed there that whole day. In the evening we were getting ready to go, but then Yosske Blinder said he wanted to go back to town to check things out: His father had a grocery store there, and he had a lot of good Polish friends. He was sure one of them might help. We decided to wait. Meanwhile we noticed there were Germans wandering about on the riverbank, close to where we were hiding. An army toilet was nearby and one of the soldiers sitting there seemed to be looking straight at us. To this day, I don't understand how he didn't see us.

A few hours later, a crestfallen Blinder was back. There was a particular gentile who owed his father a lot of money and who had lived with the Blinders as one of the family. In response to Yosske's pleas, the gentile gave Yosske a few loaves of bread and a slab of ham and sent him packing.

"Not the same world anymore," Yosske said.

We shared the food and were on our way. We went to the dock of the Jewish sports club, ŻTS, where we saw an abandoned guard post, and near it was a boat on the sandy bank. We got in and rowed to the other side, plodding in the mud until we found dry land. From there we walked along the river to a brick factory.

One of our group—I don't remember his name—served as a go-between for Sashka "Gold Teeth's" group of partisans. We would later learn that the same Sashka was a real scoundrel, a thief and a murderer, an impostor who only claimed to be a partisan leader. The underground sent groups of ten members armed with rifles and grenades with the intermediary to Sashka. Upon arrival at the destination, the intermediary would receive written confirmation from Sashka's partisans confirming that the group had arrived, and on his return, he would present the note to the underground leaders in the ghetto.

But not everything went smoothly. Each time the go-between told the Russians he wanted to speak with the previous group—as the underground had requested—the Russians would stall him with stories about how all the group members were on various missions far from the camp. After a few groups had been sent out and not heard from again, the ghetto underground became highly suspicious.

The go-between was sent alone with explicit instructions to meet with our people at any cost. Again, the Russians fed him a story that the Jews had gone on a mission and would be back the following week. He got away by promising to return the following week with two heavy machine guns. With that, all contact with the Russians was cut off and the ghetto underground did not send any more groups to the forest. We later learned that Sashka's men had murdered all the Jews who had been sent and stole their weapons and boots.

This fellow served as our guide until we reached the forest, but from there he didn't know where to go. I suggested that we divide up the weapons among us and not appoint commanders—we could manage without that —and we would start to look for the partisans. But the others asked me to take charge. We had three rifles, a lot of ammunition, bandoliers of bullets for machine guns, and hand grenades. Those of us who had army experience, including myself, took the rifles; we packed the bullets into our bandoliers and strapped them across our chests and placed the grenades in our pockets. And so we marched off feeling like real soldiers. How inexperienced we were. We didn't even know that our grenades were practice aids, completely useless.

We walked and walked for several days, tens of kilometers each day. We often lost our way, and we advanced slowly and cautiously. I walked at the lead with another fellow, and after us was the go-between. The others walked single file behind us, keeping ten meters between them. After a few such days in the forest, we ventured into a wide clearing where a shepherd was tending his sheep. We decided to stay in the area for a few days to get familiar with it and then to move on. The next morning I saw a peasant woman in the clearing looking after the sheep, so I asked one of the women in our group to go talk to her and ask her the way to Miedna, but without letting on why we wanted to know. When she returned, she had the directions.

Evening came and we walked on. A few kilometers down the road, we came upon the ruins of a few farms. The smell of fire was still in the air. The Germans must have driven the farmers from their farms to neighboring villages and then burned the farmhouses so as not to leave isolated dwellings in the forest. We went into one of the farms, looking for food. All we found was some unbaked bread dough, which we ate voraciously. We all ended up with puffy tummies, but none of us got sick. Afterward we found some beehives and scraped off some honey, ignoring the bee stings.

While we were still looking for food at the farm, I heard someone calling, "Misha! Misha! Come! Quickly!"

I ran straight over to the road near the farm and saw a few people running toward us. I shouted, "Halt! Who's there?"

The people fell to the ground in silence, too scared to speak. I could hear their heavy breathing ten meters from where I was. Three times I asked them who they were. No answer.

One of our group whispered to me in Yiddish, "Misha, what's going on. Who are they?"

The people heard the Yiddish, and they got up and called out, "Shema Yisrael! Jews!"

They ran toward us, so relieved they had found fellow Jews that they kissed and hugged us. It turned out they were refugees from the town of Domachevo. They had been working in the area while the Jews in Domachevo were murdered and were able to escape into the forest.

When the refugees heard we were headed toward Miedna, they warned us, "God forbid! There are hundreds of Germans there."

We all turned back to the forest. Fortunately, the Jews from Domachevo knew the forest as well as I knew Brisk. We told them we were trying to find partisans, and they suggested we stay where we were for the time being until things settled down a bit. They would then lead us to people who had connections with partisans. We remained there for three weeks, in a part of the forest called Staraya Kazanya. The Domachevans led us to a village where we robbed some peasants at gunpoint to get food. We even got a cow, which we slaughtered, so we had plenty of meat. But winter was coming. We needed to do something.

One of the Jews from Domachevo and two of our group went to Miedna to meet with a villager who apparently knew where we could find Sashka Gold Teeth. The three made it to the village safely, but once there were attacked by the villagers. Our men fired and the villagers ran for their lives. Then our men threw some grenades but quickly saw that they were duds—only the safety catch exploded, while the grenade itself didn't. The three finally broke off and came back.

At that point we gave up on the plan to meet the villager in Miedna, and I went with five or six others to find Sashka and his gang. On the way, close to the village of Dubica, not far from Domachevo, we ran into a motley crew: a seventy-year-old man, a thirteen-year-old boy, and two other guys, all non-Jewish. I suggested that they join us, but the old man refused.

"What good will it do us?" he asked. "We'll all be slaughtered anyway, like sheep. But not far from here is a wealthy village, Novaya Dubica. Let's go there, take the village and everything in it—cows, sheep, horses, furs, and barrels—and hide it all in the forest. Whoever makes it out alive will have enough to eat. In any case, in the winter we won't be able to make it out of the forest at all."

We liked the idea, so we all advanced toward Novaya Dubica. At that time, villagers had organized to protect their isolated villages from marauders and all sorts of violent gangs wandering around in the forests. If partisans or other bandits were spotted, the Germans would be notified at once. As soon as the villagers noticed we were surrounding the village, they rang the church bells and set stacks of hay on fire in order to signal to the Germans. We opened fire, but in truth we had no idea what to do. No one had ever taught us how to take a village. But the *sheygets* (the young thirteen-year-old rascal) knew what to do. He went into one of the houses, shot the owner with his submachine gun (he had a PPS, an excellent weapon), took a cow and a fur coat, and returned to us.

We gave up on the plan to seize the village and went back to the forest. We decided to stay there and take advantage of the new relationship we had forged with the gentiles. It paid off. The boy got us in touch with a person who had contact with Sashka. We paid that person a visit one night, at his home in one of the villages.

"Actually I haven't heard from Sashka for two weeks," he said. "The rumor is that Sashka and his group were ambushed by the Germans near the Polygon not far from Brisk. Some of his comrades were killed, but since then I have heard nothing."

It was an opportunity to get more information, so I asked him how it happened that the little sheygets became a partisan.

"The Germans had killed his whole family," said the man, "and the boy had snatched a submachine gun from one of the soldiers and escaped to the forest."

Months later this boy would become the deputy commander of the partisan unit Voroshilov.

We got back to our group at Staraya Kazanya and reported everything we had learned. We decided we would take care of ourselves and forage for food on our own. Meanwhile we heard that Sashka knew a group from Brisk was looking for him in the forest, so he and his gang of thirteen started looking for us. At that time we still didn't know how murderous they were. Only later, after we had run into them, did we hear hair-raising accounts of their exploits. The villagers said they didn't distinguish between Jews, Germans, or Belorussians—they murdered them all in cold blood.

The same day we returned from Novaya Dubica, one of our group told me he had been approached by a member of Sashka's gang. They wanted to know about the group from Brisk and suggested that we join up. The gang member left some salt and tobacco and promised that the gang would be there that same evening.

That evening they appeared, thirteen men armed with submachine guns, Sashka Gold Teeth leading them. We were very happy to see them, and they pretended to be happy, too.

We sat around the campfire and listened to their tales, and suddenly Sashka got up and said, "Guys, you are surrounded."

With that, his men grabbed their weapons and surrounded us. They herded us into the cellar of one of the burned-out farmhouses and guarded us from outside. They robbed us of everything we had—weapons, food, everything.

Then Sashka came down and said, "We know you have half a sack full of machine ammunition. Hand it over."

It was true. We had buried the sack in the ground, and I have no idea how they knew about it. In any case, we denied that we had it. They searched us bodily and found nothing.

The tension mounted, and then Ochsenboim got up and declared, "I swear a *deputat*'s [Soviet delegate's] oath that we don't have any such ammunition," and one of the other fellows swore an oath of honor as a member of the Komsomol.[4]

Sashka's response was swift.

"Get out, Comrade *Deputat*, and you, too, Comrade Komsomol," he said.

Both fellows went out, and then Sashka after them. Suddenly Sashka drew his pistol from his pocket and shot the two.

"Listen," I addressed the others. "It won't end here. Let's give them the bullets and let them choke on them. Two of us are already lying dead. We'll take off in different directions and hope they can't kill all of us at once."

We gave them what they wanted, and they promised to leave us one rifle. But naturally they left us with nothing and promised they would be back the next day.

To this day, I cannot understand why they didn't just kill all of us on the spot. In any case, they returned half an hour later. They must have realized their mistake in not killing us off. We ran off in all directions and hid in the bushes and undergrowth and heard them calling our names. They finally left and we came out of hiding, buried our dead, and swore we would give them a proper Jewish burial. It was a promise we never had the chance to keep.

Our mood was glum that night. Six weeks had passed since the liquidation of the Brisk Ghetto. November 1942 was coming to an end and winter was fast approaching. Soon it would snow. When we woke the next morning, my mind was made up. I had decided to go back to Brisk. It was impossible to stay in the forest, and if I was meant to die, better in the city where my forefathers were buried. Yosske Blinder, Sonya Greenspan, and Shmulik, a young electrician from Brisk, decided to join me. The four of us left for the city.

Brisk at that point was Judenrein. We had no problem getting into the city, and on the first night, we found shelter in the old synagogue, which had been undergoing renovations when the Russians invaded. The work had, in fact, not been completed. The floor was still half laid. The windows were boarded up. As was our method, we hid in the space between the floor and the foundations. The next night we sneaked into the ghetto, which was closed and guarded to prevent looting of any remaining property. We went into the cellar of Sonya's house, where we found a pair of boots, a kettle, and a water bucket, and we took them back to the synagogue. We removed a board from one of the windows and bent the nail holding it in place so when we left we could put it back. Yosske Blinder would go to a soup kitchen in the market that served poor workers, and he would bring back a bit of soup for us.

One time, when I left our shelter on my own to wander about and look for food, it occurred to me that I might be able to find a better place to hide. I struck up a conversation with a group of Polish women working in the area, and they agreed to hide me in one of their homes. By the next day they had lost their nerve and asked me to find another place. When night fell, I left, making my way back to the synagogue, like a shadow in the dim and empty streets. Suddenly, just ahead of me, I saw the figure of a man in a German uniform: Aushield! We passed each other in silence, and when I glanced out of the corner of my eye, I saw that he recognized me, too. I walked on but couldn't help looking back—he was looking at me, too. None of us dared to speak a word.

Three months of winter in our synagogue hiding place passed in relative calm. We lived mostly on the food Yosske brought from the soup kitchen. But that spring our good luck came to an end. One day in March 1943, a policeman living in the area discovered us: He came in through a boarded window, and from inside our shelter we heard him shake the snow from his boots. He must have noticed the place looked lived in as he immediately left to notify the police. At that moment we left and went our separate ways, having arranged a meeting place.

I spent the day hiding in outhouses. If someone knocked on the door, I moved on to the neighboring outhouse. That night, the four of us met at the designated place and found an abandoned house to hide in—in a formerly Jewish neighborhood where gypsies had been resettled. We climbed up the oven chimney pipe to the attic. We lived for six weeks in that attic until the Germans came in one day and dismantled the oven's ceramic tiles. We heard them below us, examining the oven, and we were sure they were going to climb up to the attic and find us. But they didn't, and after they left, we decided to get out of there. It was already spring, and we decided to go back to the forest.

We needed to stock up on food before we left, so I went into a grocery shop, hoping the little money we had would buy something. There was a policeman at the shop, too, and the shopkeeper served him first.

When we were alone, the shopkeeper spoke up. "Jew, go to the forest," he said. "Don't wander around here."

I naturally did not admit I was Jewish. In fact, I answered sternly, "How can you insult me like that? What made you think I am Jewish?"

I was alarmed and left the shop but went back later and asked for a few loaves of bread, a few kilos of sausage, some salt, and some tobacco. The shopkeeper wrapped it all in a bag and gave me the bill.

Then I told him I couldn't pay.

"Never mind," he said. "God will repay me. Keep safe."

* * *

Night came and we were on our way. We left the city, crossed the Mukhavets, and walked along toward the forest. We reached the brick factory at dawn, but before we managed to hide, we ran into a group of Polish workers. They noticed right away that we were Jews and immediately blocked our path and completely surrounded us. We ran furiously toward the forest, but I had an unlucky break when I stepped into a bog and my feet were steeped in the mud up to my ankles, heavy as lead. A nightmare. The Poles closed in on me and punched and hit me all over. Before I passed out, I caught sight of Blinder. He, too, had been caught, but Sonya and Shmulik managed to get away.

When I awoke, I was lying in a dimly lit warehouse, my hands and legs were tied, and I hurt all over. What hope was there? I didn't even feel the pain anymore. I felt only shock and indifference.

A crowd of gentiles were looking through the window as if they had never seen a Jew before, and shouting in Polish,

"Jews, it won't be long before the Germans come and kill you."

But then an elderly Polish man came in and seemed to take pity on us. I noticed a glimmer of humanity in his gaze, and so I beseeched him in Polish, "Holy Jesus and Maria! We are Poles. Help us get out of here."

He nodded sadly. "I can't help you," he said. "The Germans are on their way. Pray to God."

We begged him to at least untie us, which he did. He even treated us to a hand-rolled cigarette. The three of us sat and smoked for about a quarter of an hour. Outside we heard the crowd's surging excitement, and someone shouted, "The Germans are coming!"

The door burst open with a swift kick, and in the doorway stood two German soldiers holding submachine guns. For as long as I live, I will never forget that sight.

"*Juden raus! Hände hoch!* [Jews out! Hands up!]" they shouted, and we went out, our hands raised.

One of the Germans gestured with his hand to turn right, so I supposed they were going to shoot us between the trees, but when we reached the road, the Germans ordered us to keep walking. While walking, I tried to appeal to them.

"We're Poles," I said. "What do you want from us? Let us go."

But in response they swore at us, "*Jude, gehst kaput, gleich kaput* [Jew, this is the end for you, you're going to die now]."

In a while we reached the Polygon, a large camp that had been a training area for the Polish army.

We reached the gate, and then an odd thing happened to Blinder. His hair suddenly stood straight up, his eyes turned in their sockets, his hands trembled and shook violently, and he hit his head against the wall and screamed, "*Ich bin ein Jude. Schieß mir hier!* [I am a Jew! Shoot me here!"]

"Are you crazy? What's gotten into you?" I asked.

But he kept on.

"Shoot me here. I'm not going in," he said.

I tried to sway him. "We're still alive," he said. "Let's go in, spend the night, and maybe find a way out. Let's not just end it here."

He wouldn't be swayed. "No, I'm not going in," he said. "Why should I? So they can torture us? Let them shoot me here."

But the soldiers insisted that we both go inside. Blinder went berserk and I tried to calm him down.

Then I saw that his eyes looked clearer. He seemed back to normal.

We went through the gate and into the camp. On the way, Blinder said to me in Polish, "I don't know you. I have Aryan papers and I'll try to save myself."

"Fine with me," I answered, "Why not?"

We were led through a wide courtyard and into a large building. There were rooms leading off both sides of the long hallway, and German soldiers were lounging on bed boards hanging from the walls. In a vestibule at the far end of the hallway sat a German officer behind a desk, smoking a thick cigar.

The two soldiers stopped there and reported to the officer, "We brought these two Jews to be shot."

But then something totally unexpected happened. The officer gave them an angry glare and reprimanded them for "leaving their guard post in time of war."

I didn't understand everything that was said, but I understood that much, and also that the two soldiers would be punished. He dismissed them. They clicked their boots and left. The German officer then addressed us while the soldiers looked on silently from inside their rooms.

"Are you Jews?" he asked, and added other things in German.

I said nothing, and Blinder responded in fluent Polish.

"I don't understand," said the officer. "Documents!"

Blinder handed him his fake identification paper, and I took my Soviet driver's license out of my trouser pocket. The officer accepted our papers with contempt, holding them with two fingers, disgusted by even touching them, as if he were touching something filthy and contaminated.

He examined Blinder's document and read what was on the back in German: "Polish... resident of Kobryn... What is this supposed to be?"

One of the soldiers shouted from inside his room, "They should take off their pants!"

At that moment, the door opened, and in walked a

German Pole, a Volksdeutscher, who was serving as a translator.

"Hans, come here. Explain who these people are," said the officer.

I inwardly found it hopeful that he said "people" and not "Jews." But our situation was definitely perilous, as we knew that it was almost impossible to fool a Pole in such matters.

The translator came over and looked at our documents.

"What are you fellows doing here?" he asked in Polish, and Blinder fed him a story.

The man kept on asking, and Blinder kept answering, until finally the officer ran out of patience.

"Well, Hans, who are these people?" the officer asked.

"Sir," said the translator, "this fellow's father is one of the owners of the brick factory. He himself resides in Kobryn, but their house was bombed and his father was killed. Only his wife and five children survived, and now the fellow has come to sell his father's share of the factory to support his mother and siblings. The business deal went sour. One thing led to another and the other partners informed on them, that they are Jews, just to get rid of them."

It sounded to us that the translator thought we were members of the Polish resistance.

When the officer heard the tale, he was mad enough to kill.

"What were they thinking? This is not the police!" he screamed. "This is an army camp, not some damn police department! They can go to the police in Brest. Get out of here."

It was too amazing to be believed. We started in the direction of the gate when the translator suddenly appeared beside us. He blurted out in Polish, "Don't go out through the gate. Turn right and walk toward the fence until you come to an opening. You can leave from there."

We did as he advised and came to some broken planks of wood, the opening in the fence. We quickly went through and walked toward the forest. We walked along for a time in silence, trying to digest what had just happened.

After a safe enough distance, we sat down to rest and talk. Our conversation was a bit stranger than usual—we kept asking ourselves and each other if we were really alive. The whole incident had been so odd and yet wonderful— had we really been in the lion's den and come out without a scratch?

We had, and now we needed to decide what to do next. I thought we should head into the forest and try to join a group of partisans.

But Blinder suggested a madcap idea. "How about going back to Brisk and registering at the labor office so we can volunteer to work in Germany?" he asked.

"No," I said. "I can't live like you among gentiles. I'll be found. I'm going to the forest. You can do what you want."

So it was. I went into the forest and Blinder left.[5]

I wandered on my own in the forest for nearly a month. Although it was only one month, each day was like an eternity. Each day, I was sure I could no longer stand the suffering. At one place, I saw tire tracks, and when I looked around closely, I saw ditches in the sand that had been freshly dug... and scraps of paper scattered about. They looked like torn-up identification cards. I could barely make out the names on the scraps: Antonevich? Ivanson? It was hard to tell. There were also remains of food, as if someone had had a hasty meal. I realized I was standing at a site where the Nazis had massacred a few dozen Jews.

I kept walking, probably in circles. I stopped counting the days. Morning turned into night, night turned into morning. I was totally exhausted, filthy, and unshaven. At an abandoned farmhouse, I found a pile of rotted potatoes in the barn. I took off my trousers, tied the legs together, and filled the "sack" with potatoes. The potatoes jostled about inside my "sack" and turned into mush, like the mixture for making potato pancakes. At night I would fill a small tin with the mush and cook it over a fire. That was dinner. I was careful to tend the fire day and night.

Wolves roamed the area, probably feeding off the corpses, and I will never forget their howling. And their eyes. In the dark, through the trees, pairs and pairs of yellow eyes glowed like headlights. My sleep was restless. Images of Sashka and others would appear in my nightmares, all horrendous. And all around me were the corpses of the murdered. The constant walking caused my legs to swell until I could walk no further, each step too painful to bear. I lay near the fire, my whole body sore, and a blunt indifference enveloped me.

But then two figures approached. From a distance I saw they were human, but they looked strange. I lay there and watched them in amazement. On both sides of their heads, they had peculiar looking antlers and their bodies were thick at the middle as if carrying sacks on each side. When they got closer, I could see the hats they were wearing had holes on each side with their hair sticking through.

"Mishka?" one of them asked. "From Brisk? Is that you?"

"Who are you?" I asked. "Where do you know me from?"

"Don't you remember? You were with a group from Brisk when we met you. We are from Domachevo."

"What ever happened with the others?"

"They're all dead. Lying around."

I went with them to where the rest of the group was. When we got to the camp, I saw a big pot of meat cooking. Without waiting for it to be ready, I stuck my hand in and pulled out a chunk of meat and practically swallowed it whole.

I spent a few weeks with the group from Domachevo and gradually regained my strength. During the winter of 1942–43, the Germans raided the forests, and most of those in hiding perished. Few survived in the woods; others found refuge in nearby towns. Food supplies that had been prepared by the dead were used by the survivors. Every night a Russian fellow would arrive at the camp and tell us where we could find food. After I joined, the Russian started to be suspicious and stopped coming as often.

Finally, spring was there in full force and we went out to look for partisans. We would walk day and night in the forests, covering kilometers in our wanderings. One such night, I was out with two fellows from Domachevo when we heard the screeching of wagon wheels. A voice shouted to us in Russian, "Stop! Who's there?"

We came out with our hands up and saw before us a wagon and armed partisans in and around it. They were patrolling the area and led us to their wagon.

"What do you want?" asked their commander.

We answered that we wanted to join the partisans.

"Good, climb in," he said. "Comrades, give these fellows a drink."

And so we rode on in the wagon, following the patrol. The men, who were Russians, gave us samogon, bread, and pork, and we felt relaxed and revived. After a while we reached a partisan camp and a guard stopped us at the entrance. The officer in charge of the patrol ordered us to stay there and wait, which we did. An hour later we were approached by the camp commander, a guy named Vaska, and his deputy—the sheygets, the thirteen-year-old we had met the previous fall in the forest. Vaska had been wounded in the shoulder. And I noticed he carried a pistol under his coat.

"I don't take on Jews to my otriad," Vaska said.

"And why not?" I asked.

"A Jew who is caught alive always talks," he replied. "Stay here and I'll have some food sent to you. But it's impossible to let you join."

"Food is not the problem," I said. "I can get it myself. I want to fight, like you." Then, I added, "How ungrateful."

"What are you talking about?" asked Vaska. "What's it got to do with me?"

"I also had a weapon when I escaped to the forest, but I was attacked and it was stolen," I said.

"Are you from the group from Brest-Litovsk?"

"Yes."

"Well then, I know all about it," he said, and his young deputy stared at me and concluded that I did look familiar.

"I agree to accept you for a trial period," Vaska pronounced. "If after a month you have proved suitable, I will let another join, also on a trial basis. I will take on one new Jew each month."

We agreed, and so it was. I had joined a partisan camp.

Two weeks passed and nothing happened.

I approached Vaska again and asked for a weapon.

"Don't worry. That too will come," he replied.

"If that's the case, why not let the two others join? It makes no sense," I argued, and he finally agreed. Both of my friends were accepted into the camp.

It was a partisan otriad called Voroshilov, a unit about the size of a small company at that time, numbering some forty men. In those days a demolition unit, headed by a Russian who had previously been the manager of the Brisk train station. We were both from the same city, so we became rather friendly and he promised to include me in the unit. Finally, the unit was ready, and we quickly undertook our first assignment, derailing the train from Domachevo to Brisk.

We did not yet have explosives or heavy equipment. The plan was to raid the equipment shacks, overtake the guard, and take possession of the tools. Then some of the team would set about dismantling the tracks. I was given a submachine gun and stationed some two hundred meters from the team with a Russian Uzbek partisan.

The dismantling and demolishing of the tracks could be heard for quite some time. Then I suddenly saw the headlights of the train as it approached and I suggested to the Uzbek that we move back into the bushes, and if the team hadn't finished dismantling, we should open fire at the train. The Uzbek was not impressed.

"The commander stationed us here and only he can move us," he said.

I tried to argue, but it was no use.

"The commander wants us here, not there," he insisted.

We were still arguing when the train came hurtling forward at great speed, and then it suddenly flew off the tracks and rolled over. The noise was deafening. The carriage cars were dragged along and fell on each other from the elevated embankment, creating a godawful chaotic mess. In the ensuing silence, only the locomotive engine continued to clatter in rhythm.

"Let's go," shouted the Uzbek, and without waiting for an answer, he ran and jumped onto one of the overturned cars and opened the door upward. There was a group of Germans trapped inside, between the seats.

Uzbek called me, "Mishka, your weapon."

I handed it to him, and he emptied the whole magazine into the cabin car. He then nimbly jumped in and, after only a few minutes, came back out carrying a load of booty: hats, coats, pistols, watches, documents, and more.

The Uzbek seemed at ease at last, and we both turned back toward the camp. On the Domachevo-Brest-Litovsk road, we saw our comrades coming in our direction toward the train. They had left us at our post when the train was approaching, and now they were coming back to finish up the job. We told them what had happened, and we all turned back toward the camp.

On the way, the Uzbek remarked, "I'm not giving you the pistol. And no watch, either."

I hadn't asked him for anything, but I guessed he wanted to give me something. "What *are* you going to give me?" I asked.

He thought for a while and said, "The documents, the hat, and a belt."

The mood at the camp was elated. The commander assembled the whole camp and read the protocol, "On this day... the Voroshilov otriad derailed the Brest-bound train from Domachevo, causing considerable damage and many casualties."

Then he added, "Our machine gunner and his deputy, Misha Omelinski, acted with extraordinary valor. They remained at the scene of the derailment after the others had left, finishing the job."

Overnight, I had become a hero.

We gradually became more involved in partisan camp life, and soon we were indistinguishable from the others. The otriad absorbed new fighters continually and quickly grew. A small Jewish group arrived from Domachevo—

they had been wandering in the forest for some time under the leadership of Moshe Rozes, a severe man but a daring and brave fighter. Vaska decided to give them "an admissions test" and sent them to set fire to the Domachevo train station. I volunteered to go with them and help. To ensure that the operation succeeded, we received a cannon shell. The idea was to lob the shell into the fire and cause an explosion.

The operation went smoothly, without a hitch. To my surprise, the station was almost deserted—only one girl at the ticket booth. We piled hay alongside the station walls and set the station on fire. Then we threw the shell into the fire. We ran back to camp, the thunder of the explosion behind us. The partisans also heard it and Rozes' group was accepted. That brought the number of the Jews to seventeen, among dozens of Russians and Belorussians.

One day, a fellow arrived from Moscow and announced he had been sent to instruct us in the use of explosives. While he spoke, I couldn't help feeling I had met him before, but I couldn't remember from where.

We both kept looking at each other, and then it hit me: he was one of the men who worked with Sashka Gold Teeth. During the first smoking break, I rushed over to Vaska and told him about the man. We immediately set out to apprehend him, but the man had also taken advantage of the break and disappeared.

"You should have shot him on the spot," Vaska said.

* * *

In late summer 1943, while patrolling near the Bug River, we ran into a group of people wandering about. They spoke Polish, so the Russian officer asked me to translate, and at once I could tell they were Jews. But they could hardly believe that I was.

One of them remarked to his friend in Yiddish, "Is he a Jew? With a weapon? Can't be."

I communicated with them in Polish and Yiddish, and for some reason they said they wanted to cross the river west. I showed them the way and explained how the Germans guarded the border. They reconsidered and decided not to cross.

The following day, when I returned to camp, I was told that a group of Jewish partisans had arrived from west of the Bug only a few days earlier. The area was our responsibility, so to prevent them from robbing peasants, which would cause us trouble, their weapons were temporarily taken. The group was told to wait near our camp until further instructions. A few of our Jewish partisans had already visited them, and that's how I heard their leader was Moshe Lichtenberg from Włodawa. I knew Lichtenberg from the time we had both been students at the Ort school in Brisk. I then realized that the group we had met near the Bug had been sent to cross it to look for the rest of their friends, a large segment that had gotten separated and remained west, while Lichtenberg had crossed east with the others.

Meanwhile Lichtenberg set out himself to find the other group, but a few days later the first segment arrived—without their commander. It turned out that Lichtenberg had gotten caught up in a row with some Russians and been killed. Subsequently, it was decided that the Jewish partisans would advance east deep into Belorussia.

I approached Vaska and requested permission to join the Jewish group. Vaska gave me his blessing, but then the other Jews in the group, having heard, approached Vaska and asked to leave, too. Vaska assumed I had organized this little "rebellion" and went wild with rage. He stood us in a row and lashed out at us.

"Do you remember the day you arrived?" he asked, pointing to me. "You were barefoot, naked, and starving. Now you're a big hero, aren't you? Well, you can leave just the way you came."

Vaska left us with only two old rifles and sent us away.

In disgrace we left to join Lichtenberg's group. It was rather unpleasant to join them like that without weapons. Fifty of them were unarmed, and now so were we. Their group numbered about one hundred—mostly young, even children, but some older... and a few very lovely girls. There I met Sara Lustigman from Włodawa, and we soon became close friends.

I took it upon myself to guide the group, and I led them several hundred kilometers to the vicinity of Drohiczyn, across the Dnieper Canal. Our journey lasted several weeks, and when we reached our destination, we met with a senior Russian officer and requested to remain an independent Jewish unit. The officer agreed and allocated an area for us at the edge of the area under his control, near a partisan otriad that included a reconnaissance unit led by a fellow called Bezpalov (chopped finger).

Once a month, Bezpalov would give us the passcode that would enable communication between our units. The pass code was always a two-digit number, and it worked as follows: if the code was 15, and you ran into a suspicious person, you would say, "Stop, 7!" If the suspect knew the code, he would respond "8." The response was always the number you needed to add to reach 15.

We would hide the list of codes for the month in a bottle and bury it. Each day we would uncover the list and memorize the number for that day. I was assigned the job of creating a reconnaissance unit, and for that I chose the best fighters and the best weapons. Now we were ready for action.

Our first challenge was to impose our will on the villagers. We acquired horses and carts so we would be able to travel great distances fairly quickly. Then we would typically ride into a village and stop a youngster and inquire about the inhabitants. We mostly wanted to know who the Communists were and who had served prison time under the Poles. The youth would lead us to those people by describing some telling signs on their houses, and we would drop in for a visit in the early hours of the morning.

The alarmed man would be taken from his house and told that we had come from Moscow, where it was known that he was a loyal Communist. The only thing we required was that he answer a few questions. We always got the information we needed—the identities of villagers hiding weapons at home. The following nights, we would visit those houses and "talk" to them.

"Sergei, you have a machine gun and it's not doing any good, and we are losing fighters every day," we would say. "Let us have it, and if in the future you should need it, we'll give it back."

The villager would then strenuously deny owning a weapon, genuflecting and swearing on his parents' graves and by all that is holy. Then we would order him to take a shovel and come with us.

After a short distance, the villager would ask, "Where are you taking me?"

We would answer, "To dig your grave. If you prefer that your machine gun stay buried, you may as well be buried with it."

Some of the villagers needed more convincing, which took the form of beatings or even warning shots aimed near the head. The villager would invariably hand over his weapon, and thus we were able to gather almost enough weapons for everyone in the group.

We also performed certain "administrative" tasks, for example, preventing villagers from delivering the "contingent" (farm produce tax) to the Germans. To accomplish this goal, we would convene the villagers and demand that they withhold paying the contingent, to which the villagers would respond that if they did that, the Germans would retaliate and kill them. We promised to protect them, but if that didn't work, we later confiscated the contingent when it was being sent.

Once I led a group of almost one hundred on such a mission. We spread out along the road, and when the villagers approached with their eighty carts overflowing with produce, we stopped them and at gunpoint and forced them to dismount. We took the finest horses and carts and loaded geese, chickens, and samogon onto the carts, which we drove back to the camp. Bezpalov had gotten wind of it and arrived at the camp with his men to find out what was going on. We explained that we had needed to confiscate the contingent. To pacify him, we gave him twenty liters of samogon, and he left happier than ever.

We remained in that area for a few weeks, after which we burned our bridges and returned east. It was September or October 1943. We traveled east to the Dnieper Canal in the vicinity of Pinsk and entered the area controlled by the Molotov Partisan Brigade. The brigade commander received us cordially but did not permit us to remain an independent Jewish unit.

"Here we don't allow partisans to organize according to nationalities," he said. "You will be assigned to different otriads."

Thus, our group was dispersed and we were all attached to otriads in the Molotov Brigade. The Russians agreed to let families stay together. Sara and I, having said we were engaged, were assigned to the Shishov otriad, and I joined a platoon that was headed by a fellow called Popov.

We remained in that otriad until the day we were liberated. In my platoon, I was the only Jew. In Kokshin's platoon, there were four Jews, as was the case in the other platoons. The partisans (who were mostly Belorussians) usually treated us fairly, although there were occasional instances of antisemitism. I happened to be treated with respect and admiration—my commander would refer to me as "my Mishka," or he might say, "I have this Jewish fellow here, Mishka, and he's a guy you can steal horses with." They were simple folk and I won them over with my card tricks. The one case of antisemitism I recall was when a young husky Belorussian, Saborkin, threw a grenade into the zemlyanka where four Jews were living. Fortunately, the grenade didn't explode.

Another zemlyanka functioned as a logistics unit and housed a number of Jews, including a tailor, a cobbler, a seamstress, and others who provided services for the whole otriad. Most of the Jews would gather there and spend their spare time together, eating, singing, dancing, and just talking and socializing. Some of the partisans were jealous of our camaraderie and would often make stinging remarks. Others were not. On the anniversary of the October Revolution, which was a great celebration for the Soviets, everyone would get drunk on samogon and some of them would join in with the Jews.

The area of Pinsk was quite tense in those days, and the brigade functioned as a military unit in every way. Each otriad had its own base, but most of the time the combat platoons were spread throughout the area and involved in various operations, such as guarding the front line, patrolling, supervising the villagers, observing German movements, and engaging in sabotage and blowing up targets.

We would be on duty for three weeks, then replaced by another platoon and return to base for a week of "vacation." It was a military zone, a real battlefield with almost clear lines of demarcation. The Germans deployed special forces that scouted our area. They raided, harassed, and sometimes attacked viciously and methodically. Time and again we would sabotage the train tracks, and the Germans would immediately repair the damage. By late 1943 and early 1944, the German army was in full retreat along the whole front. The Red Army was advancing, and the pressure on the Germans was increasingly heavy. The greater the pressure and the closer the front, the more our presence disturbed and bothered them, and the more the Germans intensified their attacks on us.

Our demolition operations were becoming riskier as the Germans stationed armed guards at set intervals along the tracks. In one operation, we succeeded in blowing up a long track on the Brest-Litovsk–Pinsk line. The whole otriad took part, each member placing a small stick of dynamite near the track. Train transportation on that line was disrupted for months as a result.

In another operation, on a cold March night in 1944, we set out to blow up train tracks at a particular location. Previous squads had tried but failed, and our commander Kolya volunteered to do the job. Scouts led us to the location between two guard posts. Our forces spread out and secured the area from a distance, and one fellow and I went to the track and started to attach the explosive device. Snow covered the ground, and it was so cold that I blew hot air on my hands to keep my fingers from freezing. Music could be heard from a nearby village, and we imagined that the guards were distracted by the festivities, thus giving us a sense of security.

The train would arrive in a few minutes and we had to work fast. I dug under one of the wooden sleepers as I had been taught and placed the device on a sack. I then screwed the fuse in place on the bomb so that the weight of the train on the track would set it off. Lastly, I needed to pull out the safety catch and string a long wire in its place that was attached to a long string. The other end of the string was held by our men hiding not far away. The Germans protected themselves from landmine attacks by pushing a few empty cars before the locomotive. Knowing this, we needed to wait until the first cars had passed before pulling the string.

It didn't go as planned. My partner was supposed to pull the safety catch at exactly the time that I was to thread the wire, but instead of waiting, he jerked the safety catch out. I froze. It was a terrifying moment as I waited for the explosion... but the device didn't explode. My breath must have frozen the inside the mechanism, preventing it from detonating.

"Run! To the forest!" I shouted, but at that moment the train hurtled straight toward us from between the trees.

A soldier with a spotlight and machine gun was standing on the first car, watching the tracks. We rolled over in our white camouflage suits onto the embankment and covered our ears and heads. The noise of the train as it passed was deafening. The bomb didn't explode under the weight of the train.

Our operation, too, had failed. We rejoined our men and reported the foul-up. The commander ordered me to go back and dismantle the device, but I refused. It wasn't worth the risk. One of the Russians volunteered, and he managed to unscrew the fuse safely. Meanwhile rumors had reached the camp that "Mishka didn't survive the blast," and the Jews lost no time reciting prayers of mourning for the dead.

There were also battles with German forces attempting to infiltrate partisan-held territory. I vaguely remember them—only a few isolated incidents come to mind. One night, when our platoon was stationed near the Dnieper Canal, we went out to get food (each platoon took care of its own provisions when not at the base). We found an abandoned house with trenches nearby and got busy cooking and eating, all the while knowing that a large German attack was imminent. Suddenly the alarm was sounded: "To the trenches, everybody!"

Kolya didn't seem concerned. "Let's finish eating and drinking first," he said.

Suddenly all hell broke loose. We were about to go outside when we heard the barrage of machine guns, the whistle of bullets, and shrapnel. We literally jumped into the trenches when a shell hit the house, and it collapsed in a large cloud of dust.

Another time, I had just finished my "time off" at the base and joined a platoon stationed outside of the camp in a sort of dugout protected by a dirt embankment and fitted with machine-gun nests and rifle trenches. They were all sitting around shooting the breeze, and I nonchalantly sat on the embankment with my back to the enemy and started telling them about my week off and the latest gossip from the base. Suddenly a long burst of shots whizzed by, close to my ear. We jumped into the trenches and fired. The whole area suddenly came alive.

It seemed a German patrol had passed by and seen me sticking out above the embankment on the skyline. The shooting stopped after a while, but our commanders were concerned because they didn't know the location and size of the enemy forces. Orders were received from higher up to send reconnaissance to locate the Germans and estimate their strength. Each platoon sent one representative—whoever had a submachine gun—and I was sent from my platoon. Three or four men, led by an officer, set forth—advancing with great caution. There was a small graveyard near our position, and I suggested to the officer that we fire a few shots before entering. That way the Germans were likely to fire back and reveal their positions. We fired, but the Germans didn't respond. The partisans to the rear of us thought we had engaged the enemy and were all on alert and jumped into the trenches. We advanced into the graveyard.

Apparently the Germans had spotted us and were waiting for us to come within range. They had a clear view of us and opened fire. We instinctively fell to the ground and hid behind headstones, keeping low. Bullets hit the headstones, showering shrapnel and splinters. I don't remember how long the shooting lasted. It felt like hours.

But at last the firing subsided. We crawled cautiously to the left and out of the graveyard some distance and continued in the deep furrows of a recently plowed field until we reached an abandoned house. There we climbed to the roof from where we had a clear view of the area. The Germans in their shiny helmets were lying low behind shelters or in manholes, while the partisans were standing erect and moving as if they were not amid a battle. With nightfall we rejoined our forces.

The closer the Red Army got, the more the fighting intensified around us. The Dnieper Canal was the front line for quite some time, and we didn't let the Germans cross it to the south. On one occasion a sizable German force attacked our positions on the northern bank of the canal. The fighting was fierce. The Germans pressed on, and eventually we had no choice but to retreat south and they crossed the canal. But it didn't take long before they retreated again, and we regained our positions.

In March 1944, the front was only a few dozen kilometers from us. The whole German front was in retreat and the partisans in the area presented a constant danger to them. In response the Germans sent in Waffen S.S. forces, their best soldiers, to wipe out the resistance in the area. The attack was sudden and surprisingly ferocious. The enemy swiftly broke through our lines at three points and, before we had time to react, they were upon us. Our only option was to retreat south.

But in no time our orderly retreat became a rout and our units lost contact with each other. We were in flight. The villagers, too, fled in panic and the dirt roads were choked with men, women, and children, all carrying bundles and pushing carts. To make matters worse, the roads were muddy—it was still winter—and carts got stuck in the bog. The sight was pitiful, with all these people plodding through the mud or just standing, exhausted, at the roadside, barely able to move on. The Germans had blocked quite a few roads and bridges and were firing incessantly. Amid that chaos we made our way east by foot. Some of our people were killed, but to the best of my knowledge there were no Jews among them.

At some point during our retreat, a small group was sent to the base to check if anyone had remained behind and see to it that they retreat. While the others kept on, three or four of us made our way to the base—the scout officer Kolya, Avigdor Shporrer from Chelm, me, and one or two others. Near the camp I noticed studded boot tracks in the mud heading west—the Germans must have already been there.

At the camp we found the commissar and two of our women who had volunteered to bake bread for the whole otriad. To my surprise, they were Sara (my future wife) and Rivka (Avigdor's future wife). We reported to the commissar, and each of us grabbed two loaves of bread and off we left. Not far from the camp, we suddenly noticed a group of Germans. They were standing with their backs to us, checking a small wooden bridge on a stream. Someone suggested shooting them, but the commissar ordered us to move away without attracting attention. As for him, before we knew it, he had jumped on his horse and disappeared. We never saw him again.

We continued on our way along the muddy roads along with the villagers on the run. On and on we walked, all that day. The girls had a really hard time and we had to help them. Sara could barely drag her feet along but refused to let go of the bread. She finally took my advice and left it on a cart stuck at the side of the road.

With nightfall, we arrived at the area of Lake Biala Yezioro, where our otriad stopped to reorganize. But there was no time to rest. Our squad was ordered to scout and find out how far the Germans had advanced. Again, I was on duty, along with Avigdor Shporrer. We walked along forest paths all night, treading with caution. We examined each and every abandoned house but found no sign of Germans. Finally, we decided to return to the lake where our otriad was camping, but when we got there, they had all gone. They had continued retreating southeast. We did the same.

At dawn we ran into a Red Army unit. Suddenly, out of the darkness, someone shouted in Russian, "Stop! Who goes there?"

We responded with our password. They knew the drill and the password. A Soviet officer and his men emerged from behind the bushes. We briefly exchanged greetings and moved on, occasionally running into more Soviet units. The sun rose and the sky cleared. As we left the forest, we met more and more Soviet forces. We crossed a bridge on a wide stream and entered a large village. Soviet infantry and armored troops were moving north and west toward the front, while we were heading east, away from the fighting. It was early spring 1944. The sky was blue. The countryside was green. And my war was over.

A few days later, we were registered and assigned new jobs. The women stayed where they were near Kovel, which had not yet been liberated and was still being bombed. Most of the partisan fighters, aside from the most veteran, were drafted into the Red Army and sent to the front. I was sent, along with a few others, to a small village near Gomel in Belorussia. There, a Communist Party headquarters had been established, and our duty was to hand over all the "property" the partisans had accumulated—furs, horses, carts, utensils, and the like. The Russians treated us with dignity, and when our job was done, they even awarded us a few days off. Then I was summoned to headquarters and asked if I wanted to volunteer for active duty. They offered me a chance to join a commando unit that would parachute behind enemy lines. I answered that I was tired of the war and wanted to rest. The commander asked what my profession was, and I said I had been a driver before the war. So I got a job as a truck driver for the Central Committee of the Communist Party in Belorussia.

I reported for duty at a well-preserved building, and there they took my gun and sent me to a fellow named Belyakov, secretary of the local branch of the party. From there, he sent me to the garage and I started my new job as a driver. Actually I had little experience and knew nothing about mechanics, but I was a partisan, so they treated me well.

Later I drove to the partisan headquarters, a journey of three days and three nights without food or drink. When I arrived, I was given nice new clothing—part of the goods the Americans had sent their allies—a long coat, and jeans (jeans were expensive and hard to come by in Russia) and was instructed to stay there until I received my medals and payments coming to me. The salary would have been equal to four years as an army officer.

But there were so many waiting in line—thousands of people waiting days and nights—that I decided to forfeit the whole thing and I returned to my job at party headquarters. Meanwhile I took a short vacation, and Sara and I got married. We both lived in Gomel, and when the Russians liberated Minsk, we went there, and then to Pinsk. The move to Pinsk was not authorized, and once there some friends helped me get set up. From Pinsk, we went west to Brisk and in May 1945, with repatriation, we went to Włodawa, my wife's hometown.

- Misha Omelinski, Givatayim, September 1998

---

1. The testimony that Michael Omelinski gave to Yad Vashem in October 1969 can be found in their archives (0.3/3637, Yiddish).
2. Some years after my father's death, Yad Vashem got hold of a batch of application forms filled in by Jews from the Brest ghetto. I found his form among them, complete with a snapshot and personal details. But his first name on the form was Mojżesz (the Polish

version of Moshe/Moses), not Michael. I now believe his birth name was Moshe, and Misha was just what his friends called him. The name Misha stuck and was translated to Michael when he came to Israel in 1948 (YM).

3. In fact, the battle for the fortress was waged from June 22–30, 1941, when it was captured, and a mopping-up effort began. Pockets of resistance continued to fight until the end of July.

4. The Komsomol was a Leninist communist youth movement of Soviet Russia, established in 1918.

5. His son Serge says that his father didn't implement his plan. He stayed in Belorussia in hiding, and after a time, he, too, joined a group of partisans.

THE SILENT BUG

In July 2003, my mother had been invited to Poland by a German TV company (ARD), which was doing a documentary series about Jews in western Ukraine and eastern Poland, along the Bug River, during World War II. The series was entitled *Der Stille Bug* (*The Silent Bug*) since the Bug was about to become "Europe's new border" after Poland joined the European Union. Mother accepted the invitation and asked me to accompany her. At the age of seventy-nine, she was still attractive, fairly healthy, and as sharp and lucid as always. We made all the necessary arrangements and flew to Poland.

We were met at Warsaw Airport by a driver sent by the production company and driven to Włodawa. During the three-hour drive, we hardly spoke. As we made our way east, the countryside became more rural, the road narrower and pitted, and the villages sparse and neglected. Toward the end, we drove for a long time through thick forests. It was quite depressing. And although I had never been in Poland, it all looked somehow familiar.

Four years after the fall of the communist bloc, Poland was already recovering. In the big cities, one could see hectic rebuilding, and the historical monuments and quarters were undergoing a quick process of renovation. But here in the outlying areas, it seemed not much had changed in the last fifty years. The towns and villages we passed by were extremely unattractive, neglected, ravaged by time.

Włodawa was a small and quite unremarkable town in the middle of nowhere. It had an ancient town square with an ugly gray Soviet memorial, rundown shops, a few cars (most of them old), and narrow streets with dilapidated wooden houses. There were also two- and three-story apartment buildings and vacant lots scattered with heaps of junk. Here and there you could see a well-tended cottage with a flower garden or a colorful, modern building, all of which emphasized the general air of disrepair.

In contrast stood the synagogue, built in the seventeenth century, grand and beautiful and remarkably well preserved and tended. It had withstood the Nazi conquest and the Communist regime and serves today as a museum in commemoration of the Jewish community of Włodawa. The town had, of course, a large and ancient Catholic cathedral, but also a Pravoslav church, a reminder of the many Ukrainians who lived in and around the town before the war. And less than ten kilometers away was the site of the extermination camp Sobibor.

During the three days we spent there, we were filmed at all sorts of places in town—at the Lustigman family compound, near the synagogue, in the town square, and on a small bridge above a canal that Jewish slave laborers had dug during the war. My mother pointed out the places and told about her experiences. On camera, she answered questions, smiled, laughed, and cried. The interviews were held in Polish and immediately translated to German. You could feel that the production team loved her—Annette, the interviewer; Marius, the research director; Fritz, the manager; and the cameramen and technicians, too.

At the family compound, only one of the wooden houses remained. In addition, the stone flour mill still stood and was operating. My mother told about the day she and my father returned to Włodawa and the compound after the war and one of her grandfather's workers knelt and kissed her hand. Fritz, who translated to English for me, wiped away a tear. Annette cried openly.

Filming The Silent Bug, *Włodawa, 2003*

Those three days were fraught with emotion. My mother was the center of attention, and she was at her best. As for me, I felt like a foreigner, understanding neither Polish nor German, but I focused on my mother's moods. It seemed to me she was comfortable, confident, and at home as she walked about the streets. I could see how excited she was, but also how overwhelmed and sometimes sad. It's true I felt out of place, a foreigner, yet I could not rid myself of the uncanny feeling of déjà vu, that this was not new, that I had already been there.

Finally we said our goodbyes to the production crew and our driver took us back to Warsaw. On the way we passed through Lublin and visited the site of the extermination camp Majdanek. In the evening we reached Warsaw and spent another two days there as regular tourists, sightseeing, eating out, strolling through the streets, resting on park benches, and stopping for coffee. We could finally talk, and we talked a lot. I felt we had never been so close.

We were sitting on a bench in the beautiful Łazienki Park, overlooking a clear blue lake with its impressive royal palace in the center. We were resting and snacking on fruit and sandwiches.

"Why did you agree to come here?" I asked my mother. "It wasn't easy for you. I could see that. Why return and delve into painful memories?"

She was silent for a moment or two, which was unusual for her, and when she answered it was clear to me that her answer had been ready for a long time.

"True, it has not been easy," she said. "But for my whole life I have wanted my story to be told, to reach as many people as possible. They need to know. They need to understand. I don't care whether they are Poles or Germans or Israelis. The main thing is to tell the story. And one day I want you to write it."

- Yossi Millo

Sara Omelinski, 2012

Michael Omelinski, c. 1995

KIND REQUEST

Dear Reader,

If you have enjoyed reading this memoir,
please do leave a review on Amazon or Goodreads. A few
kind words would be enough. This would be greatly
appreciated.

Alternatively, if you have read this as Kindle eBook you
could leave a rating.
That is just one click, indicating how many stars of five
you think this book deserves.
This will cost you a split second.
Thank you very much in advance!

Son and daughter of the author.

HOLOCAUST SURVIVOR MEMOIRS

The Series **Holocaust Survivor Memoirs World War II** , by Amsterdam Publishers, consists of the following autobiographies of survivors:

1. Outcry - Holocaust Memoirs, by Manny Steinberg

Amazon Link: getbook.at/Outcry

2. Hank Brodt Holocaust Memoirs. A Candle and a Promise, by Deborah Donnelly

Amazon Link: getbook.at/Brodt

3. The Dead Years. Holocaust Memoirs, by Joseph Schupack

Amazon Link: getbook.at/Schupack

4. Rescued from the Ashes. The Diary of Leokadia Schmidt, Survivor of the Warsaw Ghetto, by Leokadia Schmidt

Amazon Link: getbook.at/Leokadia

5. My Lvov. Holocaust Memoir of a twelve-year-old Girl, by Janina Hescheles

Amazon Link: getbook.at/Lvov

6. Remembering Ravensbrück. From Holocaust to Healing, by Natalie Hess

Amazon Link: getbook.at/Ravensbruck

7. Wolf. A Story of Hate, by Zeev Scheinwald with Ella Scheinwald

Amazon Link: getbook.at/wolf

8. Save my Children. An Astonishing Tale of Survival and its Unlikely Hero, by Leon Kleiner with Edwin Stepp

Amazon Link: getbook.at/LeonKleiner

9. Holocaust Memoirs of a Bergen-Belsen Survivor & Classmate of Anne Frank, by Nanette Blitz Konig

Amazon Link: getbook.at/BlitzKonig

10. Defiant German - Defiant Jew. A Holocaust Memoir from inside the Third Reich, by Walter Leopold with Les Leopold

Amazon Link: getbook.at/leopold

11. In a Land of Forest and Darkness. The Holocaust Story of two Jewish Partisans, by Sara Lustigman Omelinski

Amazon Link: getbook.at/Omelinski

HOLOCAUST SURVIVOR TRUE STORIES

The Series **Holocaust Survivor True Stories WWII**, by Amsterdam Publishers, consists of the following biographies:

1. Among the Reeds. The true story of how a family survived the Holocaust, by Tammy Bottner

Amazon Link: getbook.at/ATRBottner

2. A Holocaust Memoir of Love & Resilience. Mama's Survival from Lithuania to America, by Ettie Zilber

Amazon Link: getbook.at/Zilber

3. Living among the Dead. My Grandmother's Holocaust Survival Story of Love and Strength, by Adena Bernstein Astrowsky

Amazon Link: mybook.to/ManiaL

4. Heart Songs - A Holocaust Memoir, by Barbara Gilford

Amazon Link: getbook.at/HeartSongs

5. Shoes of the Shoah. The Tomorrow of Yesterday, by Dorothy Pierce

Amazon Link: getbook.at/shoah

6. Hidden in Berlin. A Holocaust Memoir, by Evelyn Joseph Grossman

Amazon Link: getbook.at/HiddenBL

7. Separated Together. The Incredible True WWII Story of Soulmates Stranded an Ocean Apart, by Kenneth P. Price, Ph.D.

Amazon Link: getbook.at/SeparatedTG

8. The Man Across the River: The incredible story of one man's will to survive the Holocaust, by Zvi Wiesenfeld

Amazon Link: getbook.at/ZviWi

9. If Anyone Calls, Tell Them I Died. A Memoir, by Emanuel (Manu) Rosen

Amazon Link: getbook.at/EMrosen

10. The House on Thrömerstrasse. A Story of Rebirth and Renewal in the Wake of the Holocaust, by Ron Vincent

Amazon Link: getbook.at/RVincent

11. Dancing with my Father. His hidden past. Her quest for truth. How Nazi Vienna shaped a family's identity, by Jo Sorochinsky

Amazon Link: getbook.at/DancingJS

12. The Story Keeper. Weaving the Threads of Time and Memory, a Memoir, by Fred Feldman

Amazon Link: getbook.at/StoryKeeper

13. Krisia's Silence. The Girl who was not on Schindler's List, by Ronny Hein

Amazon Link: getbook.at/Krisia

14. Defying Death on the Danube. A Holocaust Survival Story, by Debbie J. Callahan with Henry Stern

Amazon Link: getbook.at/Danube

Forthcoming

15. There was a Garden in Nuremberg, by Navina Michal Clemerson

Printed in Great Britain
by Amazon

18517277R00153